DRAMA CLASSIC

The Drama Classics series aims to offer the world's greatest plays in affordable paperback editions for students, actors and theatregoers. The hallmarks of the series are accessible introductions, uncluttered texts and an overall theatrical perspective.

Given that readers may be encountering a particular play for the first time, the introduction seeks to fill in the theatrical/historical background and to outline the chief themes rather than concentrate on interpretational and textual analysis. Similarly the play-texts themselves are free of footnotes and other interpolations: instead there is an end-glossary of 'difficult' words and phrases.

The texts of the English-language plays in the series have been prepared taking full account of all existing scholarship. The foreign-language plays have been newly translated into a modern English that is both actable and accurate: many of the translators regularly have their work staged professionally.

Edited until his early death by Kenneth McLeish, the Drama Classics series continues with his aim of providing a first-class library of dramatic literature representing the best of world theatre.

Associate editors:
Professor Trevor R. Griffiths
*Visiting Professor in Humanities, Universities of Essex and
    Hertfordshire*
Dr Colin Counsell
*School of Humanities, Arts and Languages,
    London Metropolitan University*

DRAMA CLASSICS *the first hundred*

The Alchemist
All for Love
Andromache
Antigone
Bacchae
Bartholomew Fair
The Beaux Stratagem
The Beggar's Opera
Birds
Blood Wedding
Celestina
The Changeling
A Chaste Maid in Cheapside
The Cherry Orchard
Children of the Sun
El Cid
The Country Wife
The Dance of Death
The Devil is an Ass
Doctor Faustus
A Doll's House
Don Juan
The Duchess of Malfi
Edward II
Electra (Euripides)
Electra (Sophocles)
An Enemy of the People
Everyman
Faust
A Flea in her Ear
Frogs
Fuente Ovejuna
The Game of Love and Chance
Ghosts
The Government Inspector
Hecuba
Hedda Gabler

The Hypochondriac
The Importance of Being Earnest
An Ideal Husband
An Italian Straw Hat
Ivanov
The Jew of Malta
The Knight of the Burning Pestle
The Lady from the Sea
The Learned Ladies
Lady Windermere's Fan
Life is a Dream
London Assurance
The Lower Depths
The Lucky Chance
Lulu
Lysistrata
The Malcontent
The Man of Mode
The Marriage of Figaro
Mary Stuart
The Master Builder
Medea
The Misanthrope
The Miser
Miss Julie
A Month in the Country
Oedipus
The Oresteia
Peer Gynt
Phedra
The Playboy of the Western World
The Recruiting Officer
The Revenger's Tragedy
The Rivals

The Roaring Girl
La Ronde
Rosmersholm
The Rover
Scapino
The School for Scandal
The Seagull
The Servant of Two Masters
She Stoops to Conquer
The Shoemakers' Holiday
Six Characters in Search of an Author
The Spanish Tragedy
Spring Awakening
Summerfolk
Tartuffe
Three Sisters
'Tis Pity She's a Whore
Too Clever by Half
Ubu
Uncle Vanya
Volpone
The Way of the World
The White Devil
The Wild Duck
A Woman of No Importance
Women Beware Women
Women of Troy
Woyzeck
Yerma

The publishers welcome suggestions for further titles

DRAMA CLASSICS

THE KNIGHT OF THE BURNING PESTLE

by
Francis Beaumont

edited and introduced by
Colin Counsell

NICK HERN BOOKS
London
www.nickhernbooks.co.uk

A Drama Classic

This edition of *The Knight of the Burning Pestle* first published in Great Britain as a paperback original in 2001 by Nick Hern Books Limited, The Glasshouse, 49a Goldhawk Road, London W12 8QP

Reprinted 2010, 2014

Copyright in this edition of the text © 2001 Colin Counsell

Copyright in the introduction © 2001 Nick Hern Books

Typeset by Country Setting, Kingsdown, Kent CT14 8ES
Printed and bound in Great Britain by Mimeo Ltd, Huntingdon, Cambridgeshire PE29 6XX

A CIP catalogue record for this book is available from the British Library

ISBN 978 1 85459 624 6

Introduction

Francis Beaumont (1584-1616)

The son and grandson of judges, Francis Beaumont joined
the Inner Temple in London at age sixteen, intent, one
might suppose, on a career in law. Yet within a few years
his sights were firmly set on writing, and his first play, *The
Woman Hater*, was performed circa 1607. It was probably in
the same year that he first encountered John Fletcher, the
two young men reputedly having been introduced by the
dramatist Ben Jonson. Their meeting was to prove
providential, for the pair went on to form one of the most
successful playwrighting partnerships of the day, producing
such works as *Cupid's Revenge* (1608), *The Coxcomb* (1608-9), *A
King and No King* (1611), *Philaster* (1609) and, most notably
perhaps, *The Maid's Tragedy* (1610). Until quite recently
more than fifty works were attributed to Beaumont and
Fletcher jointly. Today, however, critical opinion favours the
view that Beaumont, who retired from London and from
the theatre in 1613, participated in the writing of only
twelve or fifteen of those plays.

In addition to collaborative works, both writers were to pen
dramas separately, Beaumont's corpus including his *Masque
of the Inner Temple and Gray's Inn* (1613) and, of course, *The
Knight of the Burning Pestle*. For a time the latter was thought
also to be the product of collaboration but recent linguistic
analysis suggests it is the work of Beaumont alone. It is
upon this drama that much of Beaumont's current

reputation rests. This is partly due to the play's craftsman-like qualities – its rounded characterisations, sophisticated satire and bold, measured verse, all of which are consistent characteristics of Beaumont's writing. But the play stands out most of all for its self-reflexivity, its witty interrogation of the mechanisms of theatre itself which is unsurpassed in the theatre of the English Renaissance.

What Happens in the Play

The spectators are assembled, the speaker of the prologue is about to set the scene for the scheduled play, 'The London Merchant', when the Citizen interrupts from the audience. For seven years, he complains, the theatre has staged plays ridiculing London tradesmen such as him, and, to judge from its title, that evening's entertainment is to be no different. The company should stage a different kind of work, he declares, something 'notably in honour of the commons of the city'. This drama's hero should be of his own trade, a grocer, and do heroic, grocerly deeds; he should, the Citizen's Wife suggests, kill a lion with a pestle. When the prologue speaker objects that they have no one to play such a role, since all the company have already been cast, the Citizen volunteers his wife's man, Rafe, for the part; when he explains that the company cannot afford appropriate music, the Citizen offers to pay for a band. Faced with such inducements – such *finances* – the speaker cannot resist, even permitting the Citizen and his wife to take seats on the stage so that they may watch the work unfold at close quarters.

So the audience is offered two dramas instead of one. The first is the comedy originally scheduled for performance, 'The London Merchant'. This is the story of Jasper, penniless apprentice to the merchant Venturewell, and his attempts to win the hand of the woman he loves, his master's daughter Luce. As Luce has been promised by her father to the wealthy but foolish Humphrey, the young lovers elope, undergoing ordeals and learning various lessons before finally they are granted the right to wed. The show's second thread is the tale of the heroic grocer demanded by the Citizen, the 'Knight of the Burning Pestle'. This is intended to be a drama of high romance, of knights and damsels and daring deeds. But Rafe makes a rather implausible hero, at turns clichéd and incompetent, and his status as courtly knight seems to rest largely on his determination to call women 'damsels' and horses 'palfreys'. As the show proceeds the two stories intertwine, the different fictional worlds clashing, with results that are as illuminating as they are funny.

And all the while the Citizen and his wife watch from the stage, offering advice to the characters, complaining about performances and spectators smoking, and generally inter-rupting the show. Unsophisticated and inexperienced in the ways of the theatre, they often misunderstand what is taking place, liking the villains and despising the heroes, and failing to grasp the distinction between reality and fiction. They, as much as the characters of the two plots, are a part of the entertainment, their foolishness and innocence providing an apt and comic commentary on all that takes place.

Comedy of London

The play which the actors initially propose to stage, 'The London Merchant', bears the hallmarks of a 'citizen comedy', a dramatic genre very popular in early seventeenth-century England. Citizen comedies are invariably set in London or some urban equivalent. Shakespeare's *The Merry Wives of Windsor* (c.1597), arguably the earliest example of the genre, is set in the town of the title – then a hub of trade and industry – while the events of Ben Jonson's *Bartholomew Fair* (1614) take place on the streets of the capital city itself. The urban location of the plays is often reflected in their pace and tone, with frenetic action and earthy, rapid-fire dialogue giving the feel of a bustling, commercial centre. The defining feature of such dramas is their characters, however, for citizen comedies have at their heart people of the middle and trading classes, those who, in London, held the status of freemen citizens or 'cits'.

The play's urban setting is also vital in establishing the context for its action. In the countryside of seventeenth-century England the old, essentially medieval social hierarchy of aristocracy, merchants and toiling classes was still largely in place. In this relatively static society, those born into a certain social position tended to stay within it. But the cities of the Renaissance, founded on trade, offered the chance of financial advancement, and hence social mobility. It was there, then, that notions of personal worth became detached from given social position, becoming instead a function of individual achievement; in the city, it was believed, a man might better himself armed with no more than his wits and a capacity for hard work. Ideas such as these underpin the action of 'The London Merchant'. The very assumption that an apprentice might prove a worthy match for a rich merchant's daughter demonstrates a belief in the value of personal worth over inherited position, and Jasper's triumph over his master Venturewell is essentially a victory of the young and able over the old, established and rich.

If citizen comedies revel in the possibilities for advancement offered by urban society, they also criticise it for its greed. In rejecting Jasper as a potential son in law because he lacks wealth, the merchant Venturewell demonstrates his preoccupation with money, a love of riches so great that he is willing to endanger his daughter's future happiness. A similar critique is evident in the plot concerning Jasper's father and mother, Master and Mistress Merrythought. Old Master Merrythought, we learn, has spent all his wealth and is destitute, no longer able to support his wife and second son; when she discovers this, Mistress Merrythought, who has hoarded her money, deserts him. To a modern eye Merrythought's actions may seem inexplicable, and his wife's reaction quite understandable. But Jasper's father has a symbolic significance in the play far greater than his minimal role in the plot, for he stands as the antithesis of the grasping materialism of London. Happily singing all day despite his poverty, he embodies the possibility of a carefree life, one governed by values other than a love of wealth.

Sex and the Romance

'The London Merchant' is only half the drama, of course, and the other half, the play within the play that is 'The Knight of the Burning Pestle', is a medieval romance. Romances in book form were also very popular in Renaissance England, their accounts of knights errant who humbled villains and rescued damsels appealing to a large readership. Yet this readership was mainly among the merchant and trading classes, people like the Citizen and his wife, who, although literate and affluent enough to buy books for pleasure, were unschooled in the aesthetics of 'higher' literary forms such as poetry or Greek and Roman classics. Indeed, the medieval romance genre was considered gauche by the cultural elites of the time, a thing of superficial sentiment and cheap escapism, so that in demanding such a tale be staged, the Citizen and his wife demonstrate their lack of taste. Beaumont in effect mocks them as *nouveau riche*, representatives of a citizen class that has acquired wealth but not discernment.

The adventures of Rafe are not to be taken seriously, however, for while he often quotes from the genuine heroic tales available at the time, his own story is clearly a mock romance. Not a knight at all, its hero is a questing grocer, and the damsel in whose honour he performs his daring deeds is Susan, the cobbler's daughter. 'Barbaroso', a villain with whom he does battle, is in reality the local barber, his 'tortures' no more than medical procedures which barber-surgeons commonly undertook at the time. The noble 'Knight of the Order of the Bell' is the innkeeper of The Bell public house, as becomes apparent when he demands that his 'guest', Rafe, settle his bill.

But if Beaumont works to parody the romance, he does so in order to reveal a reality behind the image. For scholar and novelist C.S. Lewis the medieval romance genre was shaped by the particular social circumstances surrounding its emergence. Feudal lords in medieval Europe, he argued, usually numbered unmarried men among their retainers, the second and third sons of other lords, who, inheriting no land, could not afford homes and families of their own. Without the means to marry, such men would choose as focus for their desires the wives of their liege lords, the only women in the vicinity of suitable social status. Feudal halls and courts were therefore marked by a peculiar situation, men identifying erotically with precisely those women who would always be beyond their reach. It was this situation, Lewis argued, which encouraged the development of a kind of literature that, while it had male-female relations at its centre, depicted those relations as emphatically chaste. The deeds undertaken by the questing knight, the obstacles he overcame and the ordeals he endured, thus symbolised a displaced, thwarted sexuality, its object of desire forever sought but never attained.

The work in which Lewis set out this thesis, *The Allegory of Love*, is now half a century old, and we may today consider it somewhat sweeping in its assumptions, reducing the complexities of an entire genre to a more or less direct reflection of social circumstances. Yet even if his theory does not offer a complete explanation, it does successfully highlight the paradox of a literary form which has male-female relationships at its heart but denies those relationships a sexual dimension. Whereas the romance proper masks that sexuality, however, Beaumont brings it to the surface, for Rafe's adventures are packed with sexual allusions. Described as 'the knight who wears [his] pestle in honour of all ladies', it is implied that he has a sexual relationship with the Citizen's Wife; when she almost lost a child, we are told, Rafe volunteered to provide her with another. His final marshalling of the London militia is filled with *double entendres*, with talk of 'touch-holes' and a 'piece' that has been shot 'partly to scour her and partly for audacity', and 'horns' reminiscent of those the cuckold was supposed to wear. With such allusions the play brings the high sentiments of the romance down to earth, its vision of an ethereal, chaste love placed alongside one which is undeniably physical.

This physical side to love is nowhere more evident than in the aftermath of Rafe's overthrow of the 'villainous' Barbaroso. Freed from the depths of his 'dungeon', his former prisoners describe in detail the tortures to which they have been subjected – the 'dieting' and 'sweating', the intravenous application of 'broth' and cutting of gristle from the nose. Such procedures may sound bizarre today but in the seventeenth century they would have been immediately recognisable as remedies for venereal disease, the kinds of treatments commonly provided by barber-surgeons. As well as mocking the literary tastes of the Citizen and his wife, the scene offers a grimly humorous reminder of what was sometimes the real penalty for illicit love, directing a not-so-gentle jab at the prettified literary genre which masked that reality.

The Comedy within the Comedy

'The London Merchant' and Rafe's tale do not comprise the whole of the entertainment, of course, for the Citizen and his wife also prove a rich source of humour. At the very outset the worthy grocer demonstrates his ignorance of those codes of behaviour proper to the theatre, interrupting the prologue speaker to complain of the fare on offer. This continues throughout, as he and his spouse remark on the action, complain about the paucity of scenes featuring their beloved Rafe, and talk to the actors onstage. If their love of the romance reveals a philistinism deemed typical of London 'cits', such behaviour demonstrates an ignorance which is its counterpart.

Both these qualities are matched by their naivety. Although the romantic lover Jasper is clearly the hero of the main plot, the Citizen and his wife prefer the doltish Humphrey, and take his part throughout. Similarly, while despising Jasper's father, the amiable spendthrift Master Merrythought, they heartily approve of his mercenary mother, and of the grasping merchant Venturewell. This suggests more than naivety, of course, for it reveals their purely mercantile view of the world. Though a fool, Humphrey is wealthy, a far better match for Luce than the penurious Jasper, while Mistress Merrythought's thrift in hoarding her money, and her decision to desert her husband when he has spent his, is testament to her financial ruthlessness. In locating their sympathies with these characters, the Citizen and his wife betray their own venality.

But the Citizen and his wife prove most eccentric when it comes to the very interpretation of events onstage. The wife, we learn, was 'ne'er at one of these plays, as they say, before' and, like her husband, proves unable to distinguish between fiction and reality. When Tim the apprentice, in the role of Rafe's squire, fails to use the correct mode of introduction for his 'knight', the Citizen berates him for his forgetfulness, as if he were not an actor and his lines were not scripted, while his wife turns to other spectators as witnesses to the boy's poor memory. Later she corrects Mistress Merrythought as if she were a real person, asserting that her 'son' did not leave Venturewell's employment voluntarily but was discharged. Indeed, when it appears that Jasper will win Luce's hand after all, the Citizen goes so far as to threaten to bring in 'half a dozen good fellows' to rectify the matter with force. Albeit that they commissioned the drama, the Citizen and his wife slip between recognising it as fiction and viewing it as if it were real, matching their unlikely response to characters to a failure to understand the basic principles of theatrical pretence.

Such play at the borders of illusion is of course a feature of the theatre of the time. The dramas of the English Renaissance are filled with plays within plays, characters who take on disguises and enact roles, and tragic protagonists who, like Hamlet and Richard III, view themselves as 'actors' on the stage of life. But in *The Knight of the Burning Pestle* such features are made to reflect the work's central themes. The romance's masking of sexuality, Rafe's unwitting parody of that genre, the citizens' misreading of the heroes as villains, and of the fictional as real – all these involve misperception, the characters' misinterpretation of their world. By including his 'audience' in the play itself, and having that audience misread the performance, Beaumont incorporates this theme into the very form of the drama, reminding the real audience that they too are viewing fictional events as if they were real.

English Theatre and the Renaissance

The Renaissance in Britain was a time of massive change and growth. In the sixteenth and seventeenth centuries a series of bad harvests and market fluctuations irreparably damaged the old land-based economy by bankrupting smallholders, whose lands were then gathered up into larger estates. One result was a steady migration from the country into the towns; it is estimated that in the 1530s London had a population of approximately fifty thousand, whereas little more than a hundred years later it was in excess of half a million. The city in which Beaumont's play was performed was a fast-expanding, crowded place, with a far more frenetic pace of life than the countryside, where many of its new inhabitants would have been born.

The Renaissance was also a time of exploration, with English traders and colonisers venturing into Asia, Africa and the New World, returning to their homeland and establishing London as a world centre of commerce. This new mercantilism affected all levels of life: the rich were richer than ever, and the poor poorer. This would have been particularly evident in a choked metropolis such as London, where different social classes were not yet separated into different communal areas and the 'high' rubbed shoulders with the 'low' on a daily basis. For Londoners of the seventeenth century, the rampant materialism displayed by such as Venturewell and Mistress Merrythought would have been more than a humorous fiction.

In their own period writers like Beaumont and Shakespeare had nothing like the status they do today, and creating theatre, or even attending it, was considered a morally dubious pastime. From the Middle Ages there stemmed a tradition of the Devil as *fals semblant*, the one who adopts pleasing disguises to lure souls into damnation. In the sixteenth century Elizabeth I introduced 'sumptuary' laws forbidding her subjects to wear clothes deemed unsuitable to their social class. Pretending to be someone else, then, was an activity viewed with mistrust in Renaissance England, and one consequence was that play performances were banned within the confines of the City of London itself. Theatres congregated in areas such as Shoreditch and the South Bank of the river Thames, within reach of the city but beyond its walls, and therefore outside its jurisdiction. In these areas other 'suspect' activities took place, such as prostitution, cockfighting and bear-baiting, and theatre companies sometimes employed the same venues. Drama was not considered an art form but a form of entertainment.

Commercial theatres in early seventeenth-century London took two forms. We are today perhaps most familiar with the so-called 'public' amphitheatres such as the Globe. These were large, polygonal structures, open to the skies, where performances took place during the day, making use of natural light. Their large stages were thrust into the space's central well with spectators positioned all around, and in galleries on the theatre building's walls. These theatres accommodated very large audiences, estimated as between two and three thousand, and were probably attended by all levels of London society. Less familiar perhaps are the 'private' theatres. Located indoors, these used smaller, end-on stages and staged their performances at night, the playing area being lit artificially. The audiences too were considerably reduced – as little as six or seven hundred according to some scholars – and were drawn from a narrower section of society. Whereas admission to the cheapest area in the public amphitheatres, the standing space of the pit, was one penny, entrance to private theatres seems to have cost at least sixpence.

First performed circa 1607-8, *The Knight of the Burning Pestle* was written for a venue of the second kind, the private Blackfriars Theatre, built in a former Dominican monastery and named after the region of London in which it was located. This did much to shape the play. The higher admission fee charged by such theatres meant that their audiences tended to be wealthier, and so were likely to have benefited from greater education than the rest of London's population, and to have enjoyed more free time that could be devoted to cultural pursuits. Such factors inevitably impacted on their tastes, and on the artworks created to satisfy them. Plays written for private theatres show a preference for irony and sophisticated satire, and relatively little liking for the sentiment, spectacle and grand heroism characteristic of many works written for the public stage. The dramas also suggest a delight in parodic play with the conventions of dramatic forms. Well schooled in the motifs of revenge tragedy, say, or history plays, such audiences could enjoy seeing those conventions thrown into ironic relief. It is therefore not incidental that *The Knight of the Burning Pestle* lampoons the crude heroism and implausible fantasy of contemporary romances, and mocks those citizens who so enjoyed them.

An equally pronounced influence was probably exerted on Beaumont's play by the kind of company for which it was written. *The Knight of the Burning Pestle* was most likely created for the Children of the Queen's Revels, a 'coterie company' composed entirely of young boys. Such troupes went through periods of great popularity in the late sixteenth and early seventeenth centuries, sometimes even threatening the income of adult companies. Moreover their playing had a particular effect, for with children or adolescents in the roles of adults, the dramas were rendered satirical. A twelve year old playing an aging king or fierce warrior inevitably threw into relief the conventions via which such characters were usually depicted. As a result tragedies and comedies seemed to reflect upon their own genres, becoming in some sense *about* tragedy or comedy. Of all the extant plays of the period, *The Knight of the Burning Pestle* is perhaps the greatest example of this, providing a meditation on the nature of dramatic representation for an audience whose tastes already predisposed them to knowing, sophisticated readings.

For Further Reading

Andrew Gurr's *The Shakespearean Stage 1574-1642*
(Cambridge University Press 1970) is perhaps the best work
on English Renaissance theatre accessible to the general
reader, but J.L. Styan's *Shakespeare's Stagecraft* (Cambridge
University Press 1967) is also very good, illustrating its
points by reference to Shakespeare's plays. Julia Briggs's
*This Stage-Play World: English Literature and its Background 1580-
1625* (Oxford University Press 1983) offers a detailed but
readable exploration of the themes found in Renaissance
plays. Brian Gibbons's *Jacobean City Comedy* (Methuen 1980)
is the standard work on comedy of this kind and addresses
Beaumont's work in detail. Keith Wrightson's *English Society
1580-1680* (Hutchinson 1982) is a general introduction to
the period and considers the emergence of that new urban
trading class depicted in the play. Christopher Hill,
however, is probably the greatest historian of seventeenth
century England. All of his works are compelling but his
The Century of Revolution (Routledge 1961) and *Liberty Against
the Law* (Penguin 1996) will perhaps be of most interest to
the reader of Beaumont's play.

THE KNIGHT OF THE BURNING PESTLE

Prologue

Where the bee can suck no honey, she leaves her sting
behind, and where the bear cannot find origanum to heal his
grief, he blasteth all other leaves with his breath. We fear it is
like to fare so with us, that seeing you cannot draw from our
labours sweet content, you leave behind you a sour mislike,
and with open reproach blame our good meaning because
you cannot reap the wonted mirth. Our intent was at this
time to move inward delight, not outward lightness, and to
breed, if it might be, soft smiling, not loud laughing, knowing
it to the wise to be a great pleasure to hear counsel mixed
with wit, as to the foolish to have sport mingled with rudeness.
They were banished the theatre of Athens, and from Rome
hissed, that brought parasites on the stage with apish actions,
or fools with uncivil habits, or courtesans with immodest
words. We have endeavoured to be as far from unseemly
speeches to make your ears glow as we hope you will be free
from unkind reports, or, mistaking the author's intention, who
never aimed at any one particular in this play, to make our
cheeks blush. And thus I leave it, and thee to thine own
censure, to like or dislike. *Vale.*

4

Dramatis Personae.

THE PROLOGUE SPEAKER
A CITIZEN
THE CITIZEN'S WIFE
RAFE, *her man*
VENTUREWELL, *a rich merchant*
JASPER, *his apprentice*
HUMPHREY, *a friend to Venturewell*
LUCE, *Venturewell's daughter*
MISTRESS MERRYTHOUGHT, *Jasper's mother*
MICHAEL, *second son of Mistress Merrythought*
OLD MERRYTHOUGHT, *Jasper's father*
TIM, *an apprentice who plays the role of a squire*
GEORGE, *an apprentice who plays the role of a dwarf*
TAPSTER
BOY that dances and sings
HOST
BARBER
THREE KNIGHTS
CAPTAIN
SERGEANT
SOLDIERS
WILLIAM HAMERTON, *a pewterer*
GEORGE GREENGOOSE, *a poulterer*
POMPIONA, *daughter to the King of Moldavia*

Induction

Several gentlemen seated on the stage. The CITIZEN, *his* WIFE *and* RAFE *seated among the audience.*

Enter the PROLOGUE SPEAKER.

PROLOGUE. From all that's near the court, from all that's great
　　Within the compass of the city walls
　　We now have brought our scene.

　　[*The* CITIZEN *ascends to the stage.*]

CITIZEN. Hold your peace, goodman boy.

PROLOGUE. What do you mean, sir?

CITIZEN. That you have no good meaning. These seven years there hath been plays at this house, I have observed it, you have still girds at citizens, and now you call your play *The London Merchant*. Down with your title, boy, down with your title.

PROLOGUE. Are you a member of the noble city?

CITIZEN. I am.

PROLOGUE. And a freeman?

CITIZEN. Yea, and a grocer.

PROLOGUE. So, grocer, then by your sweet favour, we intend no abuse to the city.

CITIZEN. No, sir? Yes, sir! If you were not resolved to play the jacks, what need you study for new subjects purposely

to abuse your betters? Why could not you be contented, as
well as others, with *The Legend of Whittington*, or *The Life and
Death of Sir Thomas Gresham, with the Building of the Royal
Exchange*? Or *The Story of Queen Elenor, with the Rearing of
London Bridge upon Wool Sacks*?

PROLOGUE. You seem to be an understanding man. What
would you have us do, sir?

CITIZEN. Why, present something notably in honour of the
commons of the city.

PROLOGUE. Why, what do you say to *The Life and Death of
Fat Drake*, or *The Repairing of Fleet Privies*?

CITIZEN. I do not like that, but I will have a citizen and he
shall be of my own trade.

PROLOGUE. Oh, you should have told us your mind a
month since. Our play is ready to begin now.

CITIZEN. 'Tis all one for that. I will have a grocer and he
shall do admirable things.

PROLOGUE. What will you have him do?

CITIZEN. Marry, I will have him –

WIFE [*from below*]. Husband, husband!

RAFE [*from below*]. Peace, mistress.

WIFE. Hold thy peace, Rafe, I know what I do, I warrant ye.
Husband, husband!

CITIZEN. What sayst thou, cony?

WIFE. Let him kill a lion with a pestle, husband, let him kill
a lion with a pestle.

CITIZEN. So he shall. I'll have him kill a lion with a pestle.

WIFE. Husband, shall I come up, husband?

CITIZEN. Ay, cony. Rafe, help your mistress this way. Pray, gentlemen, make her a little room. I pray you, sir, lend me your hand to help up my wife. I thank you, sir. So.

[*His* WIFE *is helped onto the stage.*]

WIFE. By your leave, gentlemen all, I'm something troublesome. I'm a stranger here. I was ne'er at one of these plays, as they say, before. But I should have seen *Jane Shore* once and my husband hath promised me any time this twelvemonth to carry me to *The Bold Beauchamps*, but in truth he did not. I pray you bear with me.

CITIZEN. Boy, let my wife and I have a couple of stools, and then begin, and let the grocer do rare things.

PROLOGUE. But sir, we have never a boy to play him, every one hath a part already.

WIFE. Husband, husband, for God's sake, let Rafe play him. Beshrew me if I do not think he will go beyond them all.

CITIZEN. Well remembered, wife. Come up, Rafe. I'll tell you, gentlemen, let them but lend him a suit of reparel and necessaries, and, by gad, if any of them all blow wind in the tail on him, I'll be hanged.

WIFE. I pray you youth, let him have a suit of reparel. I'll be sworn, gentlemen, my husband tells you true. He will act you sometimes at our house that all the neighbours cry out on him. He will fetch you up a couraging part so in the garret that we are all as feared, I warrant you, that we quake again. We'll fear our children with him if they be never so unruly. Do but cry, 'Rafe comes, Rafe comes', to them and they'll be as quiet as lambs. Hold up thy head, Rafe; show the gentlemen what thou canst do. Speak a huffing part. I warrant you, the gentlemen will accept of it.

CITIZEN. Do, Rafe, do.

RAFE. By heaven, methinks it were an easy leap
   To pluck bright honour from the pale-faced moon,
   Or dive into the bottom of the sea
   Where never fathom line touched any ground,
   And pluck up drowned honour
   From the lake of hell.

CITIZEN. How say you, gentlemen? Is it not as I told you?

WIFE. Nay, gentlemen, he hath played before, my husband
   says; Mucedorus before the wardens of our company.

CITIZEN. Ay, and he should have played Jeronimo with a
   shoemaker for a wager.

PROLOGUE. He shall have a suit of apparel if he will go in.

CITIZEN. In Rafe, in Rafe, and set out the grocers in their
   kind, if thou lovest me.

   [*Exit* RAFE.]

WIFE. I warrant our Rafe will look finely when he's dressed.

PROLOGUE. But what will you have it called?

CITIZEN. *The Grocer's Honour.*

PROLOGUE. Methinks *The Knight of the Burning Pestle* were
   better.

WIFE. I'll be sworn, husband, that's as good a name as can
   be.

CITIZEN. Let it be so. Begin, begin, my wife and I will sit
   down.

PROLOGUE. I pray you do.

CITIZEN. What stately music have you? You have shawms?

PROLOGUE. Shawms? No.

CITIZEN. No? I'm a thief if my mind did not give me so.
Rafe plays a stately part and he must needs have shawms.
I'll be at the charge of them myself rather than we'll be
without them.

PROLOGUE. So you are like to be.

CITIZEN. Why and so I will be. There's two shillings. Let's
have the waits of Southwark. They are as rare fellows as
any are in England, and that will fetch them all o'er the
water with a vengeance, as if they were mad.

PROLOGUE. You shall have them. Will you sit down then?

CITIZEN. Ay. Come, wife.

WIFE. Sit you merry all, gentlemen. I'm bold to sit amongst
you for my ease.

[*They all sit.*]

PROLOGUE.
From all that's near the court, from all that's great
Within the compass of the city walls,
We now have brought our scene. Fly far from hence
All private taxes, immodest phrases,
Whate'er may but show like vicious,
For wicked mirth never true pleasure brings,
But honest minds are pleased with honest things.
Thus much for that we do: but for Rafe's part, you must
answer for yourself.

CITIZEN. Take you no care for Rafe. He'll discharge
himself, I warrant you.

WIFE. I'faith, gentlemen, I'll give my word for Rafe.

ACT ONE

Enter VENTUREWELL *and* JASPER.

VENTUREWELL.
    Sirrah, I'll make you know you are my prentice,
    And whom my charitable love redeemed
    Even from the fall of fortune; gave thee heat
    And growth to be what now thou art, new cast thee;
    Adding the trust of all I have at home,
    In foreign staples, or upon the sea
    To thy direction; tied the good opinions
    Both of self and friends to thy endeavours:
    So fair were thy beginnings. But with these
    As I remember, you had never charge
    To love your master's daughter, and even then,
    When I had found a wealthy husband for her,
    I take it, sir, you had not. But, however,
    I'll break the neck of that commission,
    And make you know you are but a merchant's factor.

JASPER. Sir, I do liberally confess I am yours,
    Bound both by love and duty to your service,
    In which my labour hath been all my profit.
    I have not lost in bargain, nor delighted
    To wear your honest gains upon my back,
    Nor have I given a pension to my blood,
    Or lavishly in play consumed your stock.
    These, and the miseries that do attend them,
    I dare with innocence proclaim are strangers
    To all my temperate actions. For your daughter,

If there be any love to my deservings,
Borne by her virtuous self, I cannot stop it.
Nor am I able to refrain her wishes.
She's private to herself and best of knowledge
Whom she'll make so happy as to sigh for.
Besides, I cannot think you mean to match her
Unto a fellow of so lame a presence,
One that hath little left of nature in him.

VENTUREWELL. 'Tis very well, sir, I can tell your wisdom
How all this shall be cured.

JASPER.   Your care becomes you.

VENTUREWELL.
And thus it shall be, sir. I here discharge you
My house and service. Take your liberty,
And when I want a son I'll send for you.

[*Exit* VENTUREWELL.]

JASPER. These be the fair rewards of them that love.
Oh, you that live in freedom never prove
The travel of a mind led by desire.

[*Enter* LUCE.]

LUCE. Why, how now, friend? Struck with my father's
thunder?

JASPER. Struck, and struck dead, unless the remedy
Be full of speed and virtue. I am now
What I expected long, no more your father's.

LUCE. But mine.

JASPER.   But yours and only yours, I am.
That's all I have to keep me from the statute.
You dare be constant still?

LUCE.   Oh, fear me not.
In this I dare be better than a woman.
Nor shall his anger, nor his offers move me,
Were they both equal to a prince's power.

JASPER. You know my rival?

LUCE.   Yes and love him dearly,
Even as I love an ague or foul weather.
I prithee, Jasper, fear him not.

JASPER.   Oh, no,
I do not mean to do him so much kindness.
But to our own desires; you know the plot
We both agreed on?

LUCE.   Yes, and will perform
My part exactly.

JASPER.   I desire no more,
Farewell, and keep my heart. 'Tis yours.

LUCE.   I take it.
He must do miracles makes me forsake it.

[*Exit both.*]

CITIZEN. Fie upon 'em, little infidels. What a matter's
here now? Well, I'll be hanged for a halfpenny if there be
not some abomination knavery in this play. Well, let 'em
look to't. Rafe must come and if there be any tricks
a-brewing –

WIFE. Let 'em brew and bake too, husband, a God's name.
Rafe will find all out, I warrant you, and they were older
than they are.

[*Enter* BOY.]

I pray my pretty youth, is Rafe ready?

BOY. He will be presently.

WIFE. Now I pray you make my commendations unto him and withal carry him this stick of liquorice. Tell him his mistress sent it him, and bid him bite a piece. 'Twill open his pipes the better, say.

[*Enter* VENTUREWELL *and* MASTER HUMPHREY.]

VENTUREWELL.
Come, sir, she's yours, upon my faith she's yours,
You have my hand. For other idle lets
Between your hopes and her, thus, with a wind
They are scattered and no more. My wanton prentice,
That like a bladder blew himself with love,
I have let out, and sent him to discover
New masters yet unknown.

HUMPHREY.   I thank you, sir,
Indeed I thank you, sir, and ere I stir
It shall be known however you do deem,
I am of gentle blood and gentle seem.

VENTUREWELL. Oh, sir, I know it certain.

HUMPHREY.   Sir, my friend,
Although, as writers say, all things have end,
And that we call a pudding hath his two,
Oh, let it not seem strange, I pray to you,
If in this bloody simile I put
My love, more endless than frail things or gut.

WIFE. Husband, I prithee, sweet lamb, tell me one thing, but tell me truly – stay youths, I beseech you, till I question my husband.

CITIZEN. What is it, mouse?

WIFE. Sirrah, didst thou ever see a prettier child? How it
behaves itself, I warrant ye, and speaks and looks and perts
up the head? I pray you, brother, with your favour, Were
you never none of Master Moncasters scholars?

CITIZEN. Chicken, I prithee heartily, contain thyself. The
childer are pretty childer, but when Rafe comes, lamb –

WIFE. Ay, when Rafe comes, cony – Well, my youth, you
may proceed.

VENTUREWELL.
Well, sir, you know my love, and rest, I hope,
Assured of my consent. Get but my daughter's
And wed her when you please. You must be bold
And clap in close unto her. Come, I know
You have language good enough to win a wench.

WIFE. A whoreson tyrant! Hath been an old stringer in his
days, I warrant him.

HUMPHREY. I take your gentle offer, and withal
Yield love again for love reciprocal.

[*Enter* LUCE.]

VENTUREWELL. What, Luce, within there?

LUCE. Called you, sir?

VENTUREWELL. I did
Give entertainment to this gentleman
And see you be not froward. To her, sir.
My presence will but be an eyesore to you.

[*Exit* VENTUREWELL.]

HUMPHREY. Fair Mistress Luce, how do you? Are you well?
    Give me your hand and then, I pray you, tell
    How doth your little sister and your brother.
    And whether you love me or any other.

LUCE. Sir, these are quickly answered.

HUMPHREY.   So they are,
    Where women are not cruel. But how far
    Is it now distant from the place we are in
    Unto that blessed place, your father's warren?

LUCE. What makes you think of that, sir?

HUMPHREY.   Even that face.
    For, stealing rabbits whilom in that place,
    God Cupid or the keeper, I know not whether,
    Unto my cost and charges brought you thither,
    And there began –

LUCE.   Your game, sir.

HUMPHREY.   Let no game
    Or any thing that tendeth to the same
    Be evermore remembered, thou fair killer,
    For whom I sat me down and brake my tiller.

WIFE. There's a kind gentleman, I warrant you. When will
    you do as much for me, George?

LUCE. Beshrew me, sir, I am sorry for your losses,
    But as the proverb says, I cannot cry.
    I would you had not seen me.

HUMPHREY.   So would I,
    Unless you had more maw to do me good.

LUCE. Why, cannot this strange passion be withstood?
    Send for a constable and raise the town.

HUMPHREY. Oh no, my valiant love will batter down
    Millions of constables and put to flight
    even that great watch of Midsummer day at night.

LUCE. Beshrew me, sir, 'twere good I yielded then.
    Weak women cannot hope where valiant men
    Have no resistance.

HUMPHREY. Yield then, I am full
    Of pity, though I say it, and can pull
    Out of my pocket thus a pair of gloves.
    Look, Lucy, look, the dog's tooth nor the dove's
    Are not so white as these, and sweet they be,
    And whipped about with silk, as you may see.
    If you desire the price, shoot from your eye
    A beam to this place, and you shall espy
    F. S., which is to say, my sweetest honey,
    They cost me three and two pence, or no money.

LUCE. Well, sir, I take them kindly, and I thank you.
    What would you more?

HUMPHREY.   Nothing.

LUCE.   Why then, farewell.

HUMPHREY. Nor so, nor so, for, lady, I must tell
    Before we part, for what we met together.
    God grant me time and patience, and fair weather.

LUCE. Speak and declare your mind in terms so brief.

HUMPHREY. I shall. Then first and foremost for relief
    I call to you, if that you can afford it.
    I care not at what price, for, on my word, it
    Shall be repaid again although it cost me
    More than I'll speak of now. For love hath tossed me
    In furious blanket like a tennis ball,
    And now I rise aloft, and now I fall.

LUCE. Alas, good gentleman, alas the day.

HUMPHREY. I thank you heartily and, as I say,
     Thus do I still continue without rest,
     I'th' morning like a man, at night a beast,
     Roaring and bellowing mine own disquiet,
     That much I fear, forsaking of my diet,
     Will bring me presently to that quandary,
     I shall bid all adieu.

LUCE.   Now, by Saint Mary,
     That were great pity.

HUMPHREY.   So it were, beshrew me.
     Then ease me, lusty Luce, and pity show me.

LUCE. Why, sir, you know my will is nothing worth
     Without my father's grant. Get his consent
     And then you may with assurance try me.

HUMPHREY. The worshipful your sire will not deny me,
     For I have asked him and he hath replied,
     'Sweet Master Humphrey, Luce shall be thy bride.'

LUCE. Sweet Master Humphrey, then I am content.

HUMPHREY. And so am I, in truth.

LUCE.   Yet take me with you.
     There is another clause must be annexed,
     And this it is I swore, and will perform it;
     No man shall ever joy me as his wife
     But he that stole me hence. If you dare venture,
     I am yours. You need not fear, my father loves you.
     If not, farewell for ever.

HUMPHREY.   Stay, nymph, stay!
     I have a double gelding, coloured bay,
     Sprung by his father from Barbarian kind,

Another for my self, though somewhat blind,
Yet true as trusty tree.

LUCE.   I am satisfied,
And so I give my hand, our course must lie
Through Waltham Forrest, where I have a friend
Will entertain us. So farewell, Sir Humphrey.
And think upon your business.

[*Exit* LUCE.]

HUMPHREY.   Though I die,
I am resolved to venture life and limb
For one so young, so fair, so kind, so trim.

[*Exit* HUMPHREY.]

WIFE. By my faith and troth, George, and as I am virtuous,
it is e'en the kindest young man that ever trod on shoe
leather. Well, go thy ways, if thou hast her not, 'tis not thy
fault, i'faith.

CITIZEN. I prithee, mouse, be patient. 'A shall have her or
I'll make some of 'em smoke for't.

WIFE. That's my good lamb, George. Fie, this stinking
tobacco kills men. Would there were none in England.
Now I pray, Gentlemen, what good does this stinking
tobacco do you? Nothing, I warrant. You make chimneys
o' your faces. Oh, husband, husband, now, now there's
Rafe, there's Rafe.

[*Enter* RAFE, *like a grocer in his shop, with two apprentices,* TIM
and GEORGE, *reading* Palmerin of England.]

CITIZEN. Peace, fool, let Rafe alone. Hark you, Rafe, do
not strain yourself too much at the first. Peace! Begin,
Rafe.

RAFE (*reads*). 'Then Palmerin and Trineus, snatching their
lances from their dwarfs and clasping their helmets,
galloped amain after the giant, and Palmerin, having
gotten a sight of him, came posting amain, saying, "Stay,
traitorous thief, for thou mayst not so carry away her that
is worth the greatest lord in the world"; and with these
words gave him a blow on the shoulder, that he struck him
besides his elephant; and Trineus, coming to the knight
that had Agricola behind him, set him soon besides his
horse, with his neck broken in the fall, so that the princess,
getting out of the throng, between joy and grief, said,
"All happy knight, the mirror of all such as follow arms,
now may I be well assured of the love thou bearest me."'
I wonder why the kings do not raise an army of fourteen
or fifteen hundred thousand men, as big as the army that
the Prince of Portigo brought against Rosicleer, and
destroy these giants? They do much hurt to wandering
damsels that go in quest of their knights.

WIFE. Faith, husband, and Rafe says true, for they say the
King of Portugal cannot sit at his meat but the giants and
the ettins will come and snatch it from him.

CITIZEN. Hold thy tongue. On, Rafe.

RAFE. And certainly those knights are much to be
commended, who, neglecting their possessions, wander with
a squire and a dwarf through the deserts to relieve poor
ladies.

WIFE. Ay, by my faith, are they, Rafe. Let 'em say what they
will, they are indeed. Our knights neglect their possessions
well enough but they do not the rest.

RAFE. There are no such courteous and fair, well-spoken
knights in this age. They will call one 'the son of a whore'
that Palmerin of England would have called 'fair sir', and

one that Rosicleer would have called 'right beautiful
damsel' they will call 'damned bitch'.

WIFE. I'll be sworn will they, Rafe. They have called me so
an hundred times about a scurvy pipe of tobacco.

RAFE. But what brave spirit could be content to sit in his
shop with a flappet of wood and a blue apron before him,
selling mithridatum and dragon's water to visited houses,
that might pursue feats of arms and through his noble
achievements procure such a famous history to be written
of in his heroic prowess?

CITIZEN. Well said, Rafe. Some more of those words, Rafe.

WIFE. They go finely, by my troth.

RAFE. Why should I not then pursue this course, both for
the credit of myself and our company? For amongst all the
worthy books of achievements, I do not call to mind that I
yet read of a grocer errant. I will be the said knight. Have
you heard of any that hath wandered unfurnished of his
squire and dwarf? My elder prentice Tim shall be my
trusty squire and little George my dwarf. Hence my blue
apron! Yet in remembrance of my former trade, upon my
shield shall be portrayed a burning pestle, and I will be
called the Knight of the Burning Pestle.

WIFE. Nay, I dare swear thou wilt not forget thy old trade.
Thou wert ever meek.

RAFE. Tim.

TIM. Anon.

RAFE. My beloved squire and George my dwarf, I charge
you that from henceforth you never call me by any other
name but the 'Right Courteous and Valiant Knight of the
Burning Pestle', and that you never call any female by the

name of a woman or wench but 'fair lady', if she have her
desires, if not, 'distressed damsel'; that you call all forests
and heaths 'deserts', and all horses 'palfries'.

WIFE. This is very fine, faith. Do the gentlemen like Rafe,
think you, husband?

CITIZEN. Ay. I warrant thee, the players would give all the
shoes in their shop for him.

RAFE. My beloved squire Tim, stand out. Admit this were a
desert and over it a knight errant pricking, and I should
bid you inquire of his intents, what would you say?

TIM. Sir, my master sent me to know whither you are riding?

RAFE. No, thus; 'Fair sir, the Right Courteous, and Valiant
Knight of the Burning Pestle commanded me to enquire
upon what adventure you are bound, whether to relieve
some distressed damsel or otherwise'.

CITIZEN. Whoreson blockhead cannot remember!

WIFE. I'faith, and Rafe told him on't before, all the
gentlemen heard him. Did he not, gentlemen? Did not
Rafe tell him on't?

GEORGE. Right Courteous and Valiant Knight of the
Burning Pestle, here is a distressed damsel, to have a
halfpenny worth of pepper.

WIFE. That's a good boy. See, the little boy can hit it. By my
troth, it's a fine child.

RAFE. Relieve her with all courteous language. Now shut up
shop, no more my prentice but my trusty squire and
dwarf. I must bespeak my shield and arming pestle.

[*Exit* TIM *and* GEORGE.]

CITIZEN. Go thy ways, Rafe. As I am a true man, thou art
the best on 'em all.

WIFE. Rafe, Rafe.

RAFE. What say you, mistress?

WIFE. I prithee come again quickly, sweet Rafe.

RAFE. By and by.

[*Exit* RAFE.]

[*Enter* JASPER *and his mother,* MISTRESS
MERRYTHOUGHT.]

MISTRESS MERRYTHOUGHT. Give thee my blessing?
No, I'll never give thee my blessing, I'll see thee hanged
first. It shall ne'er be said I gave thee my blessing. Thou
art thy father's own son, of the blood of the Merrythoughts.
I may curse the time that e'er I knew thy father. He hath
spent all his own and mine too, and when I tell him of it,
he laughs and dances and sings, and cries, 'A merry heart
lives long-a'. And thou art a waste-thrift, and art run away
from thy master that loved thee well, and art come to me,
and I have laid up a little for my younger son, Michael,
and thou thinkst to bezzle that, but thou shalt never be
able to do it.

[*Enter* MICHAEL.]

Come hither, Michael. Come, Michael, down on thy knees.
Thou shalt have my blessing.

MICHAEL. I pray you, mother, pray to God to bless me.

MISTRESS MERRYTHOUGHT. God bless thee – but
Jasper shall never have my blessing. He shall be hanged
first, shall he not, Michael? How sayest thou?

MICHAEL. Yes, forsooth, mother, and grace of God.

MISTRESS MERRYTHOUGHT. That's a good boy.

WIFE. I'faith, it's a fine spoken child:

JASPER. Mother, though you forget a parent's love,
I must preserve the duty of a child.
I ran not from my master, nor return
To have your stock maintain my idleness.

WIFE. Ungracious child, I warrant him. Hark how he chops
logic with his mother. Thou hadst best tell her she lies. Do,
tell her she lies.

CITIZEN. If he were my son, I would hang him up by the
heels and flay him and salt him, whoreson halter-sack!

JASPER. My coming only is to beg your love,
Which I must ever, though I never gain it,
And howsoever you esteem of me,
There is no drop of blood hid in these veins
But I remember well belongs to you
That brought me forth, and would be glad for you
To rip them all again and let it out.

MISTRESS MERRYTHOUGHT. I'faith, I had sorrow
enough for thee, God knows, but I'll hamper thee well
enough. Get thee in, thou vagabond, get thee in and learn
of thy brother Michael.

[*Exit* JASPER *and* MICHAEL.]

OLD MERRYTHOUGHT [*sings, within*].
Nose, nose, jolly red nose,
And who gave thee this jolly red nose?

MISTRESS MERRYTHOUGHT. Hark, my husband, he's
singing and hoiting, and I'm fain to cark and care, and all
little enough. Husband, Charles, Charles Merry-thought!

[*Enter* OLD MERRYTHOUGHT.]

OLD MERRYTHOUGHT [*sings*].
Nutmegs and ginger, cinamon and cloves,
And they gave me this jolly red nose.

MISTRESS MERRYTHOUGHT. If you would consider
your estate, you would have little list to sing, iwis.

OLD MERRYTHOUGHT. It should never be considered
while it were an estate if I thought it would spoil my
singing.

MISTRESS MERRYTHOUGHT. But how wilt thou do,
Charles? Thou art an old man and thou canst not work,
and thou hast not forty shillings left, and thou eatest good
meat and drinkest good drink, and laughest?

OLD MERRYTHOUGHT. And will do.

MISTRESS MERRYTHOUGHT. But how wilt thou come
by it, Charles?

OLD MERRYTHOUGHT. How? Why, how have I done
hitherto these forty years? I never came into my dining-
room but at eleven and six o'clock I found excellent meat
and drink o'th'table. My clothes were never worn out but
next morning a tailor brought me a new suit – and
without question it will be so ever! Use makes perfectness.
If all should fail, it is but a little straining myself
extraordinary, and laugh myself to death.

WIFE. It's a foolish old man this, is not he, George?

CITIZEN. Yes, cony.

WIFE. Give me a penny i'th'purse while I live, George.

CITIZEN. Ay, by lady, cony, hold thee there.

MISTRESS MERRYTHOUGHT. Well, Charles, you
promised to provide for Jasper and I have laid up for
Michael. I pray you, pay Jasper his portion. He's come
home and he shall not consume Michael's stock. He says
his master turned him away but I promise you truly,
I think he ran away.

WIFE. No, indeed, Mistress Merrythought, though he be a
notable gallows yet I'll assure you his master did turn him
away, even in this place. 'Twas, i'faith, within this half
hour, about his daughter. My husband was by.

CITIZEN. Hang him, rogue, he served him well enough.
Love his master's daughter! By my troth, cony, if there
were a thousand boys, thou wouldst spoil them all with
taking their parts. Let his mother alone with him.

WIFE. Ay, George, but yet truth is truth.

OLD MERRYTHOUGHT. Where is Jasper? He's welcome
however. Call him in, he shall have his portion. Is he
merry?

[*Enter* JASPER *and* MICHAEL.]

MISTRESS MERRYTHOUGHT. Ay, foul chive him, he is
too merry. Jasper! Michael!

OLD MERRYTHOUGHT. Welcome, Jasper, though thou
run'st away, welcome, God bless thee. 'Tis thy mother's
mind thou shouldst receive thy portion. Thou hast been
abroad and I hope hast learnt experience enough to
govern it – thou art of sufficient years. Hold thy hand:
one, two, three, four, five, six, seven, eight, nine, there is
ten shillings for thee. Thrust thyself into the world with
that and take some settled course. If fortune cross thee,
thou hast a retiring place; come home to me, I have
twenty shillings left. Be a good husband, that is, wear

ordinary clothes, eat the best meat and drink the best
drink, be merry, and give to the poor, and believe me,
thou hast no end of thy goods.

JASPER. Long may you live free from all thought of ill,
And long have cause to be thus merry still.
But father –

OLD MERRYTHOUGHT. No more words, Jasper, get thee
gone, thou hast my blessing. Thy father's spirit upon thee.
Farewell, Jasper. [*Sings.*]
But yet, or ere you part, oh cruel,
Kiss me, kiss, me sweeting, mine own dear jewel.
So, now begone, no words.

[*Exit* JASPER.]

MISTRESS MERRYTHOUGHT. So, Michael, now get thee
gone too.

MICHAEL. Yes forsooth, Mother, but I'll have my father's
blessing first.

MISTRESS MERRYTHOUGHT. No, Michael, 'tis no
matter for his blessing, thou hast my blessing. Begone. I'll
fetch my money and jewels and follow thee. I'll stay no
longer with him, I warrant thee. Truly, Charles, I'll be
gone too.

OLD MERRYTHOUGHT. What, you will not?

MISTRESS MERRYTHOUGHT. Yes, indeed will I.

OLD MERRYTHOUGHT [*sings*].
Hey-ho, farewell, Nan,
I'll never trust wench more again, if I can.

MISTRESS MERRYTHOUGHT. You shall not think when
all your own is gone to spend that I have been scraping up

for Michael.

OLD MERRYTHOUGHT. Farewell, good wife, I expect it
not. All I have to do in this world is to be merry, which I
shall, if the ground be not taken from me. And if it be,
[*Sings.*]
When earth and seas from me are reft,
The skies aloft for me are left.

[*Exit.*]

[Interlude]

Boy danceth. Music.

WIFE. I'll be sworn he's a merry old gentleman, for all that.
Hark, hark, husband, hark, fiddles, fiddles! Now surely they
go finely. They say 'tis present death for these fiddlers to
tune their rebecks before the Great Turk's grace, is't not,
George? But look, look, here's a youth dances. Now, good
youth, do a turn o'th'toe. Sweetheart, i'faith, I'll have Rafe
come and do some of his gambols. He'll ride the wild
mare, gentlemen, 'twould do your hearts good to see him.
I thank you, kind youth, pray bid Rafe come.

CITIZEN. Peace, cony. Sirrah, you scurvy boy, bid the
players send Rafe or by God's – and they do not, I'll tear
some of their periwigs beside their heads: this is all riff-raff.

ACT TWO

Enter VENTUREWELL *and* HUMPHREY.

VENTUREWELL. And how, faith, how goes it now, son
  Humphrey?

HUMPHREY. Right worshipful, and my beloved friend
  And father dear, this matter's at an end.

VENTUREWELL. 'Tis well, it should be so. I'm glad the girl
  Is found so tractable.

HUMPHREY.   Nay, she must whirl
  From hence, and you must wink – for so, I say,
  The story tells – tomorrow before day.

WIFE. George, dost thou think in thy conscience now 'twill
  be a match? Tell me but what thou think'st, sweet rogue.
  Thou seest the poor gentleman, dear heart, how it labours
  and throbs, I warrant you, to be at rest. I'll go move the
  father for't.

CITIZEN. No, no, I prithee, sit still, honeysuckle, thou'lt spoil
  all. If he deny him, I'll bring half a dozen good fellows
  myself and, in the shutting of an evening, knock't up, and
  there's an end.

WIFE. I'll buss thee for that, i'faith, boy. Well, George, well,
  you have been a wag in your days, I warrant you. But
  God forgive you, and I do with all my heart.

VENTUREWELL.
  How was it, son? You told me that tomorrow
  Before day break, you must convey her hence.

HUMPHREY. I must, I must, and thus it is agreed.
    Your daughter rides upon a brown-bay steed,
    I on a sorrel, which I bought of Brian,
    The honest host of the Red Roaring Lion
    In Waltham situate. Then if you may,
    Consent in seemly sort, lest by delay
    The fatal sisters come and do the office,
    And then you'll sing another song.

VENTUREWELL.   Alas.
    Why should you be thus full of grief to me,
    That do as willing as your self agree
    To anything, so it be good and fair?
    Then steal her when you will, if such a pleasure
    Content you both. I'll sleep and never see it,
    To make your joys more full. But tell me why
    You may not here perform your marriage?

WIFE. God's blessing o'thy soul, old man. I'faith, thou art
    loath to part true hearts. I see 'a has her, George, and I'm
    as glad on't. Well, go thy ways, Humphrey, for a fair-
    spoken man. I believe thou hast not thy fellow within the
    walls of London; and I should say the suburbs too, I
    should not lie. Why dost not thou rejoice with me, George?

CITIZEN. If I could but see Rafe again, I were as merry as
    mine host, i'faith.

HUMPHREY. The cause you seem to ask, I thus declare –
    Help me, oh muses nine – your daughter sware
    A foolish oath, the more it was the pity.
    Yet none but my self within this city
    Shall dare to say so, but a bold defiance
    Shall meet him, were he of the noble science.
    And yet she sware, and yet why did she swear?
    Truly I cannot tell, unless it were

For her own ease. For sure, sometimes an oath,
Being sworn, thereafter is like cordial broth.
And this it was she swore: never to marry
But such a one whose mighty arm could carry
– As meaning me, for I am such a one –
Her bodily away through stick and stone
Till both of us arrive, at her request,
Some ten miles off in the wide Waltham Forest.

VENTUREWELL. If this be all, you shall not need to fear
Any denial in your love. Proceed.
I'll neither follow, nor repent the deed.

HUMPHREY. Good night, twenty good nights, and twenty more,
And twenty more good nights, that makes threescore.

[*Exit.*]

[*Enter* MISTRESS MERRYTHOUGHT, *carrying a jewel casket and purse, and her son* MICHAEl.]

MISTRESS MERRYTHOUGHT. Come, Michael, art thou not weary, boy?

MICHAEL. No, forsooth, mother, not I.

MISTRESS MERRYTHOUGHT. Where be we now, child?

MICHAEL. Indeed, forsooth, mother, I cannot tell, unless we be at Mile End. Is not all the world Mile End, mother?

MISTRESS MERRYTHOUGHT. No, Michael, not all the world, boy – but I can assure thee, Michael, Mile End is a goodly matter. There has been a pitch-field, my child, between the naughty Spaniels and the Englishmen, and the Spaniels ran away, Michael, and the Englishmen followed. My neighbor, Coxstone, was there, boy, and killed them all with a birding piece.

MICHAEL. Mother, forsooth.

MISTRESS MERRYTHOUGHT. What says my white boy?

MICHAEL. Shall not my father go with us too?

MISTRESS MERRYTHOUGHT. No, Michael, let thy father go snick up. He shall never come between a pair of sheets with me again while he lives. Let him stay at home and sing for his supper, boy. Come, child, sit down, and I'll show my boy fine knacks indeed. Look here, Michael, here's a ring and here's a brooch, and here's a bracelet, and here's two rings more, and here's money, and gold by th'eye, my boy.

MICHAEL. Shall I have all this, mother?

MISTRESS MERRYTHOUGHT. Ay, Michael thou shalt have all, Michael.

CITIZEN. How likest thou this wench?

WIFE. I cannot tell. I would have Rafe, George, I'll see no more else indeed, la, and I pray you let the youths understand so much by word of mouth. For I will tell you truly, I'm afraid o'my boy. Come, come, George, let's be merry and wise. The child's a fatherless child, and say they should put him into a strait pair of gaskins, 'twere worse than knot-grass; he would never grow after it.

[*Enter* RAFE, TIM *dressed as a squire and* GEORGE *as a dwarf.*]

CITIZEN. Here's Rafe, here's Rafe.

WIFE. How do you, Rafe? You are welcome, Rafe, as I may say. It's a good boy, hold up thy head, and be not afraid; we are thy friends, Rafe. The gentlemen will praise thee, Rafe, if thou play'st thy part with audacity. Begin, Rafe, o'God's name.

RAFE. My trusty squire, unlace my helm, give me my hat.
    Where are we, or what desert might this be?

GEORGE. Mirror of knighthood, this is, as I take it, the
    perilous Waltham Down, in whose bottom stands the
    enchanted valley.

MISTRESS MERRYTHOUGHT. Oh Michael, we are
    betrayed, we are betrayed. Here be giants. Fly, boy, fly,
    boy, fly!

[*Exit* MOTHER *and* MICHAEL.]

RAFE. Lace on my helm again. What noise is this?
    A gentle lady flying the embrace
    Of some uncourteous knight? I will relieve her.
    Go, squire, and say the knight that wears this pestle
    In honor of all ladies swears revenge
    Upon that recreant coward that pursues her.
    Go comfort her and that same gentle squire
    That bears her company.

TIM. I go, brave knight.

RAFE. My trusty dwarf and friend, reach me my shield
    And hold it while I swear, first by my knighthood,
    Then by the soul of Amadis de Gaul,
    My famous ancestor, then by my sword
    The beauteous Brionella girt about me:
    By this bright burning pestle of mine honor,
    The living trophy, and by all respect
    Due to distressed damsels, here I vow
    Never to end the quest of this fair lady
    And that forsaken squire till by my valour
    I gain their liberty.

GEORGE. Heaven bless the knight
    That thus relieves poor errant gentlewomen.

[*Exit.*]

WIFE. Ay, marry, Rafe, this has some savour in't. I would see
the proudest of them all offer to carry his books after him.
But George, I will not have him go away so soon. I shall
be sick if he go away, that I shall. Call Rafe again,
George, call Rafe again. I prithee, sweetheart, let him
come fight before me, and let's ha' some drums and
trumpets, and let him kill all that comes near him, and
thou lov'st me, George.

CITIZEN. Peace a little, bird. He shall kill them all and they
were twenty more on 'em than there are.

[*Enter* JASPER.]

JASPER. Now, fortune, if thou be'st not only ill,
Show me thy better face and bring about
Thy desperate wheel, that I may climb at length
And stand. This is our place of meeting,
If love have any constancy. Oh age,
Where only wealthy men are counted happy,
How shall I please thee? How deserve thy smiles
When I am only rich in misery?
My father's blessing and this little coin
Is my inheritance – a strong revénue!
From earth thou art, and to earth I give thee.

[*Casts the money away.*]

There grow and multiply, whilst fresher air
Breeds me a fresher fortune.

[*Spies the casket.*]

How, illusion!
What hath the devil coined himself before me?
'Tis metal good, it rings well. I am waking,

And taking, too, I hope. Now God's dear blessing
Upon his heart that left it here, 'tis mine.
These pearls, I take it, were not left for swine.

[*Exit.*]

WIFE. I do not like that this unthrifty youth should embezzle
away the money. The poor gentlewoman his mother will
have a heavy heart for it, God knows.

CITIZEN. And reason good, sweet heart.

WIFE. But let him go. I'll tell Rafe a tale in's ear shall fetch
him again with a wanion, I warrant him, if he be above
ground. And besides, George, here be a number of
sufficient gentlemen can witness, and myself, and yourself,
and the musicians, if we be called in question. But here
comes Rafe, George. Thou shalt hear him speak as he
were an emperal.

[*Enter* RAFE *and* GEORGE.]

RAFE. Comes not Sir Squire again?

GEORGE.   Right courteous knight,
Your squire doth come, and with him comes the lady.

[*Enter* MISTRESS MERRYTHOUGHT, MICHAEL
and TIM.]

For and the Squire of Damsels, as I take it.

RAFE. Madam, if any service or devoir
Of a poor errant knight may right your wrongs,
Command it. I am prest to give you succour,
For to that holy end I bear my armour.

MISTRESS MERRYTHOUGHT. Alas, sir, I am a poor
gentlewoman and I have lost my money in this forest.

RAFE. Desert, you would say, lady, and not lost
  Whilst I have sword and lance. Dry up your tears,
  Which ill befits the beauty of that face,
  And tell the story, if I may request it,
  Of your disastrous fortune.

MISTRESS MERRYTHOUGHT. Out alas. I left a thousand
  pound, a thousand pound, e'en all the money I had laid
  up for this youth, upon the sight of your mastership, you
  looked so grim; and, as I may say it, saving your presence,
  more like a giant than a mortal man.

RAFE. I am as you are, lady, so are they
  All mortal. But why weeps this gentle squire?

MISTRESS MERRYTHOUGHT. Has he not cause to weep,
  do you think, when he has lost his inheritance?

RAFE. Young hope of valour, weep not. I am here
  That will confound thy foe, and pay it dear
  Upon his coward head that dare deny
  Distressed squires and ladies equity.
  I have but one horse, on which shall ride
  This lady fair behind me, and before
  This courteous squire; fortune will give us more
  Upon our next adventure. Fairly speed
  Beside us, squire and dwarf, to do us need.

  [*Exit.*]

CITIZEN. Did not I tell you, Nell, what your man would do?
  By the faith of my body, wench, for clean action and good
  delivery they may all cast their caps at him.

WIFE. And so they may, i'faith, for I dare speak it boldly: the
  twelve companies of London cannot match him, timber for
  timber. Well, George, and he be not inveigled by some of
  these paltery players, I ha' much marvel. But George, we
  ha' done our parts if the boy have any grace to be thankful.

CITIZEN. Yes, I warrant you, duckling.

[*Enter* HUMPHREY *and* LUCE.]

HUMPHREY. Good Mistress Luce, however I in fault am
    For your lame horse; you're welcome unto Waltham.
    But which way now to go or what to say
    I know not truly till it be broad day.

LUCE. Oh, fear not, master Humphrey, I am guide
    For this place good enough.

HUMPHREY.   Then up and ride,
    Or if it please you, walk for your repose,
    Or sit, or if you will, go pluck a rose,
    Either of which shall be indifferent
    To your good friend and Humphrey, whose consent
    Is so intangled ever to your will
    As the poor harmless horse is to the mill.

LUCE. Faith and you say the word, we'll e'en sit down
    And take a nap.

HUMPHREY.   'Tis better in the town,
    Where we may nap together, for, believe me,
    To sleep without a snatch would mickle grieve me.

LUCE. You're merry, master Humphrey.

HUMPHREY.   So I am,
    And have been ever merry from my dam.

LUCE. Your nurse had the less labour.

HUMPHREY.   Faith it may be,
    Unless it were by chance I did beray me.

[*Enter* JASPER.]

JASPER. Luce, dear friend Luce!

LUCE. Here, Jasper.

JASPER. You are mine.

HUMPHREY. If it be so, my friend, you use me fine.
What do you think I am?

JASPER. An arrant noddy.

HUMPHREY. A word of obloquy! Now, by God's body,
I'll tell thy master, for I know thee well.

JASPER. Nay, and you be so forward for to tell,
Take that and that, and tell him, sir, I gave it,
And say I paid you well.

HUMPHREY. Oh, sir, I have it,
And do confess the payment, pray be quiet.

JASPER. Go, get you to your night-cap and the diet
To cure your beaten bones.

LUCE. Alas, poor Humphrey.
Get thee some wholesome broth with sage and comfrey,
A little oil of roses and a feather
To 'noint thy back withal.

HUMPHREY. When I came hither,
Would I had gone to Paris with John Dory.

LUCE. Farewell, my pretty Nump, I am very sorry
I cannot bear thee company.

HUMPHREY. Farewell.
The devil's dam was ne'er so banged in hell.

[*Exit* LUCE *and* JASPER.]

WIFE. This young Jasper will prove me another thing, o'my
conscience, and he may be suffered. George, dost not see,

George, how 'a swaggers, and flies at the very heads o'
folks as he were a dragon? Well, if I do not do his lesson
for wronging the poor gentleman, I am no true woman.
His friends that brought him up might have been better
occupied, iwis, than have taught him these fegaries. He's
e'en in the highway to the gallows, God bless him.

CITIZEN. You're too bitter, cony. The young man may do
well enough for all this.

WIFE. Come hither, master Humphrey, has he hurt you?
Now beshrew his fingers for't. Here, sweetheart, here's
some green ginger for thee. Now beshrew my heart, but 'a
has peppernel in's head as big as a pullet's egg. Alas, sweet
lamb, how thy temples beat. Take the peace on him,
sweetheart, take the peace on him.

[*Enter a* BOY.]

CITIZEN. No, no, you talk like a foolish woman. I'll ha'
Rafe fight with him and swinge him up well-favouredly.
Sirrah boy, come hither. Let Rafe come in and fight with
Jasper.

WIFE. Ay, and beat him well. He's an unhappy boy.

BOY. Sir, you must pardon us. the plot of our play lies
contrary and 'twill hazard the spoiling of our play.

CITIZEN. Plot me no plots! I'll ha' Rafe come out! I'll make
your house too hot for you, else.

BOY. Why, sir, he shall, but if any thing fall out of order, the
gentlemen must pardon us.

CITIZEN. Go your ways, goodman boy, I'll hold him a
penny he shall have his belly full of fighting now. Ho, here
comes Rafe; no more.

[*Enter* RAFE, MISTRESS MERRYTHOUGHT,
MICHAEL, TIM *and* GEORGE.]

RAFE. What knight is that, squire? Ask him if he keep
The passage bound by love of lady fair,
Or else but prickant.

HUMPHREY. Sir, I am no knight,
But a poor gentleman that this same night
Had stolen from me on yonder green
My lovely wife, and suffered − to be seen
Yet extant on my shoulder − such a greeting
That whilst I live, I shall think of that meeting.

WIFE. Ay, Rafe, he beat him unmercifully, Rafe. And thou
sparest him, Rafe, I would thou wert hanged.

CITIZEN. No more, wife, no more.

RAFE. Where is the caitiff wretch hath done this deed?
Lady, your pardon, that I may proceed
Upon the quest of this injurious knight.
And thou, fair squire, repute me not the worse
In leaving the great venture of the purse
And the rich casket till some better leisure.

[*Enter* JASPER *and* LUCE.]

HUMPHREY. Here comes the broker hath purloined my
treasure.

RAFE. Go, squire, and tell him I am here,
An errant knight at arms, to crave delivery
Of that fair lady to her own knight's arms.
If he deny, bid him take choice of ground,
And so defy him.

TIM.   From the knight that bears
The golden pestle, I defie thee, knight,

Unless thou make fair restitution
Of that bright lady.

JASPER.   Tell the knight that sent thee
He is an ass, and I will keep the wench
And knock his head-piece.

RAFE.   Knight, thou art but dead
If thou recall not thy uncourteous terms.

WIFE. Break's pate, Rafe, break's pate, Rafe, soundly.

JASPER. Come, knight, I am ready for you. Now your pestle.

[*Snatches away his pestle.*]

Shall try what temper, sir, your mortar's of?
[*Recites.*] 'With that he stood upright in his stirrups and gave
the Knight of the Calf-skin such a knock [*He knocks* RAFE
down.] that he forsook his horse, and down he fell; and
then he leaped upon him, and plucking off his helmet – '

HUMPHREY. Nay, and my noble knight be down so soon,
Though I can scarcely go, I needs must run.

[*Exit* HUMPHREY *and* RAFE.]

WIFE. Run, Rafe, run Rafe, run for thy life, boy! Jasper
comes, Jasper comes!

JASPER. Come Luce, we must have other arms for you.
Humphrey and Golden Pestle, both adieu.

[*Exit* JASPER *and* LUCE.]

WIFE. Sure, the devil, God bless us, is in this springald. Why,
George, didst ever see such a fire-drake? I am afraid my
boy's miscarried. If he be, though he were Master
Merrythought's son a thousand times, if there be any law
in England, I'll make some of them smart for't.

CITIZEN. No, no, I have found out the matter, sweetheart:
Jasper is enchanted. As sure as we are here, he is
enchanted. He could no more have stood in Rafe's hands
than I can stand in my Lord Mayor's. I'll have a ring to
discover all enchantments, and Rafe shall beat him yet. Be
no more vexed, for it shall be so.

[*Enter* RAFE, TIM, GEORGE, MISTRESS
MERRYTHOUGHT *and* MICHAEL.]

WIFE. Oh husband, here's Rafe again. Stay, Rafe, let me
speak with thee. How dost thou, Rafe? Art thou not
shroadly hurt? The foul great lungies laid unmercifully on
thee. There's some sugar-candy for thee. Proceed, thou
shalt have another bout with him.

CITIZEN. If Rafe had him at the fencing school, if he did
not make a puppy of him and drive him up and down the
school, he should ne'er come in my shop more.

MISTRESS MERRYTHOUGHT. Truly, master Knight of
the Burning Pestle, I am weary.

MICHAEL. Indeed la, mother, and I am very hungry.

RAFE. Take comfort, gentle dame, and your fair squire,
For in this desert there must needs be placed
Many strong castles, held by courteous knights,
And till I bring you safe to one of those,
I swear by this my order ne'er to leave you.

WIFE. Well said, Rafe. George, Rafe was ever comfortable,
was he not?

CITIZEN. Yes, duck.

WIFE. I shall ne'er forget him. When we had lost our child
(you know it was strayed almost alone, to Puddle Wharf,
and the criers were abroad for it, and there it had

drowned itself but for a sculler), Rafe was the most
comfortablest to me. 'Peace mistress', says he, 'let it go. I'll
get you another as good.' Did he not, George? Did he not
say so?

CITIZEN. Yes indeed did he, mouse.

GEORGE. I would we had a mess of pottage and a pot of
drink, squire, and were going to bed.

TIM. Why, we are at Waltham town's end, and that's the Bell
Inn.

GEORGE. Take courage, valiant knight, damsel, and squire.
I have discovered, not a stone's cast off,
An ancient castle held by the old knight
Of the most holy order of the Bell,
Who gives to all knights errant entertain.
There plenty is of food, and all prepared
By the white hands of his own lady dear.
He hath three squires that welcome all his guests:
The first hight Chamberlino, who will see
Our beds prepared and bring us snowy sheets,
Where never footman stretched his buttered hams.
The second hight Tapstero, who will see
Our pots full filled, and no froth therein.
The third, a gentle squire Ostlero hight,
Who will our palfries slick with wisps of straw,
And in the manger put them oats enough,
And never grease their teeth with candle-snuff.

WIFE. That same dwarf's a pretty boy, but the squire's a
groutnoll.

RAFE. Knock at the gates, my squire, with stately lance.

[*Enter* TAPSTER.]

TAPSTER. Who's there? You're welcome, gentlemen. Will you see a room?

GEORGE. Right courteous and valiant Knight of the Burning Pestle, this is the squire Tapstero.

RAFE. Fair squire Tapstero, I, a wandering knight,
Hight of the Burning Pestle, in the quest
Of this fair lady's casket and wrought purse,
Losing my self in this vast wilderness,
And to this castle well by fortune brought,
Where hearing of the goodly entertain
Your knight of holy order of the Bell
Gives to all damsels and all errant knights,
Thought to knock, and now am bold to enter.

TAPSTER. An't please you see a chamber, you are very welcome.

[*Exit.*]

WIFE. George, I would have something done and I cannot tell what it is.

CITIZEN. What is it, Nell?

WIFE. Why George, shall Rafe beat nobody again? Prithee, sweetheart, let him.

CITIZEN. So he shall, Nell, and if I join with him, we'll knock them all.

[*Enter* HUMPHREY *and* VENTUREWELL.]

WIFE. Oh, George, here's master Humphrey again, now, that lost mistress Luce, and Mistress Luce's father. Master Humphrey will do somebody's errand, I warrant him.

HUMPHREY. Father, it's true in arms I ne'er shall clasp her,
For she is stol'n away by your man Jasper.

WIFE. I thought he would tell him.

VENTUREWELL. Unhappy that I am to lose my child.
    Now I begin to think on Jasper's words,
    Who oft hath urged to me thy foolishness,
    Why didst thou let her go, thou lov'st her not,
    That wouldst bring home thy life, and not bring her.

HUMPHREY. Father forgive me, I shall tell you true,
    Look on my shoulders, they are black and blue,
    Whilst too and fro fair Luce and I were winding,
    He came and basted me with a hedge-binding.

VENTUREWELL. Get men and horses straight, we will be there
    Within this hour. You know the place again?

HUMPHREY. I know the place where he my loins did swaddle.
    I'll get six horses, and to each a saddle.

VENTUREWELL. Meantime I'll go talk with Jasper's father.

    [*Exit.*]

WIFE. George, what wilt thou lay with me now, that Master Humphrey has not Mistress Luce yet? Speak, George, what wilt thou lay with me?

CITIZEN. No, Nell, I warrant thee, Jasper is at Puckeridge with her by this.

WIFE. Nay, George, you must consider mistress Luce's feet are tender; and besides, 'tis dark, and I promise you truly, I do not see how he should get out of Waltham Forest with her yet.

CITIZEN. Nay, cony, what wilt thou lay with me that Rafe has her not yet?

WIFE. I will not lay against Rafe, honey, because I have not spoken with him – but look, George, peace, here comes the merry old gentleman again.

[*Enter* OLD MERRYTHOUGHT.]

OLD MERRYTHOUGHT [*sings*].
When it was grown to dark midnight
And all were fast asleep,
In came Margaret's grimly ghost,
And stood at William's feet.
I have money, and meat, and drink before hand till tomorrow at noon. Why should I be sad? Methinks I have half a dozen jovial spirits within me: [*Sings.*]
I am three merry men, and three merry men.
To what end should any man be sad in this world? Give me a man that when he goes to hanging cries: [*Sings.*]
Troll the black bowl to me,
and a woman that will sing a catch in her travail. I have seen a man come by my door with a serious face, in a black cloak, without a hat band, carrying his head as if he looked for pins in the street. I have looked out of my window half a year after and have spied that man's head upon London Bridge. 'Tis vile. Never trust a tailor that does not sing at his work – his mind is of nothing but filching.

WIFE. Mark this, George, 'tis worth noting: Godfrey my tailor, you know, never sings, and he had fourteen yards to make this gown; and I'll be sworn Mistress Pennistone the draper's wife had one made with twelve.

OLD MERRYTHOUGHT [*sings*].
'Tis mirth that fills the veins with blood,
More than wine, or sleep, or food.
Let each man keep his heart at ease,
No man dies of that disease.

He that would his body keep
From diseases, must not weep,
But whoever laughs and sings,
Never his body brings
Into fevers, gouts or rheums,
Or ling'ringly his lungs consumes:
Or meets with aches in the bone,
Or catarrhs, or griping stone:
But contented lives for aye,
The more he laughs, the more he may.

WIFE. Look, George, how sayst thou by this, George? Is't not a fine old man? Now God's blessing o'thy sweet lips. When wilt thou be so merry, George? Faith, thou art the frowningst little thing when thou art angry, in a country.

[*Enter* VENTUREWELL.]

CITIZEN. Peace, cony, thou shalt see him took down too, I warrant thee. Here's Luce's father come now.

OLD MERRYTHOUGHT [*sings*].
As you came from Walsingham,
From the Holy Land,
There met you not with my true love
By the way as you came.

VENTUREWELL. Oh, Master Merrythought, my daughter's gone!
This mirth becomes you not, my daughter's gone.

OLD MERRYTHOUGHT [*sings*].
Why, an if she be, what care I?
Or let her come or go, or tarry.

VENTUREWELL. Mock not my misery. It is your son,
Whom I have made my own when all forsook him,
Has stolen my only joy, my child, away.

OLD MERRYTHOUGHT [*sings*].
  He set her on a milk white steed
  And himself upon a grey,
  He never turned his face again,
  But he bore her quite away.

VENTUREWELL. Unworthy of the kindness I have shown
  To thee, and thine. Too late I well perceive
  Thou art consenting to my daughter's loss.

OLD MERRYTHOUGHT. Your daughter? What a-stirs
  here wi' your daughter? Let her go, think no more on her,
  but sing loud. If both my sons were on the gallows, I
  would sing: [*Sings.*]
  Down, down, down they fall
  Down, and arise they never shall.

VENTUREWELL. Oh, might I behold her once again.
  And she once more embrace her aged sire.

OLD MERRYTHOUGHT. Fie, how scurvily this goes. 'And
  she once more embrace her aged sire'? You'll make a dog
  on her, will ye? She cares much for her aged sire, I
  warrant you. [*Sings.*]
  She cares not for her daddy, nor
  She cares not for her mammy.
  For she is, she is, she is my
  Lord of Lowgave's lassy.

VENTUREWELL. For this thy scorn I will pursue that son
  of thine to death.

OLD MERRYTHOUGHT. Do, and when you ha killed him:
  [*Sings.*]
  Give him flowers enow, palmer, give him flowers enow.
  Give him red and white, and blue, green, and yellow.

VENTUREWELL. I'll fetch my daughter.

OLD MERRYTHOUGHT. I'll hear no more o'your
daughter, it spoils my mirth.

VENTUREWELL. I say, I'll fetch my daughter.

OLD MERRYTHOUGHT [*sings*].
Was never man for lady's sake,
Down, down,
Tormented as I, poor Sir Guy?
De derry down,
For Luce's sake, that lady bright,
Down, down,
As ever men beheld with eye?
De derry down.

VENTUREWELL. I'll be revenged, by heaven.

[*Exit.*]

[Interlude]

Music.

WIFE. How dost thou like this, George?

CITIZEN. Why this is well, cony, but if Rafe were hot once,
thou shouldst see more.

WIFE. The fiddlers go again, husband.

CITIZEN. Ay, Nell, but this is scurvy music. I gave the
whoreson gallows money and I think he has not got me
the waits of Southwark. If I hear him not anon, I'll twinge
him by the ears. Your musicians play 'Baloo'.

WIFE. No, good George, let's ha' 'Lachrymae'.

CITIZEN. Why, this is it, cony.

WIFE. It's all the better, George. Now, sweet lamb, what story is that painted upon the cloth? The Confutation of Saint Paul?

CITIZEN. No, Lamb, that's Rafe and Lucrece.

WIFE. Rafe and Lucrece? Which Rafe? Our Rafe?

CITIZEN. No, mouse, that was a Tartarian.

WIFE. A Tartarian? Well, I would the fiddlers had done that we might see our Rafe again.

ACT III

Enter JASPER *and* LUCE.

JASPER. Come, my dear, though we have lost our way,
    We have not lost ourselves. Are you not weary
    With this night's wand'ring, broken from your rest?
    And frighted with the terror that attends
    The darkness of this wild unpeopled place?

LUCE. No, my best friend, I cannot either fear
    Or entertain a weary thought whilst you,
    The end of all my full desires, stand by me.
    Let them that lose their hopes and live to languish
    Amongst the number of forsaken lovers,
    Tell the long weary steps and number time,
    Start at a shadow and shrink up their blood,
    Whilst I, possessed with all content and quiet,
    Thus take my pretty love and thus embrace him.

JASPER. You have caught me, Luce, so fast that whilst I live
    I shall become your faithful prisoner,
    And wear these chains for ever. Come, sit down,
    And rest your body, too, too delicate
    For these disturbances. So, will you sleep?
    Come, do not be more able than you are.
    I know you are not skilful in these watches,
    For women are no soldiers. Be not nice
    But take it – sleep, I say.

LUCE.   I cannot sleep.
    Indeed I cannot, friend.

JASPER.   Why then we'll sing,
  And try how that will work upon our senses.

LUCE. I'll sing, or say, or anything but sleep.

JASPER. Come, little mermaid, rob me of my heart
  With that enchanting voice.

LUCE.   You mock me, Jasper.

Song.

JASPER.
  Tell me, dearest, what is love?

LUCE.
  'Tis a lightning from above,
  'Tis an arrow, 'tis a fire,
  'Tis a boy they call Desire.
  'Tis a smile
  Doth beguile

JASPER.
  The poor hearts of men that prove,
  Tell me more, are women true?

LUCE.
  Some love change, and so do you.

JASPER.
  Are they fair, and never kind?

LUCE.
  Yes, when men turn with the wind.

JASPER.
  Are they froward?

LUCE.
  Ever toward
  Those that love, to love anew.

JASPER. Dissemble it no more, I see the god
    Of heavy sleep lay on his heavy mace,
    Upon your eyelids.

LUCE.   I am very heavy.

[*She sleeps.*]

JASPER. Sleep, sleep, and quiet rest crown thy sweet
    thoughts:
    Keep from her fair blood distempers, startings,
    Horrors and fearful shapes. Let all her dreams
    Be joys and chaste delights, embraces, wishes,
    And such new pleasures as the ravished soul
    Gives to the senses. So, my charms have took.
    Keep her, you powers divine, whilst I contemplate
    Upon the wealth and beauty of her mind.
    She is only fair and constant, only kind,
    And only to thee, Jasper. Oh my joys,
    Whither will you transport me? Let not fullness
    Of my poor buried hopes come up together
    And overcharge my spirits. I am weak.
    Some say, however ill, the sea and women
    Are governed by the moon. Both ebb and flow,
    Both full of changes. Yet to them that know
    And truly judge, these but opinions are,
    And heresies to bring on pleasing war
    Between our tempers, that without these were
    Both void of after-love, and present fear,
    Which are the best of Cupid. Oh thou child
    Bred from despair, I dare not entertain thee,
    Having a love without the faults of women,
    And greater in her perfect goods than men;
    which to make good, and please myself the stronger,
    Though certainly I am certain of her love,

I'll try her, that the world and memory
May sing to after-times her constancy.

[*Draws his sword.*]

Luce, awake, Luce.

LUCE. Why do you fright me, friend,
With those distempered looks? What makes your sword
Drawn in your hand? Who hath offended you?
I prithee, Jasper, sleep, thou art wild with watching,

JASPER. Come make your way to heaven, and bid the world,
With all the villainies that stick upon it,
Farewell; you're for another life.

LUCE.   Oh Jasper.
How have my tender years committed evil,
Especially against the man I love,
Thus to be cropped untimely?

JASPER.   Foolish girl,
Canst thou imagine I could love his daughter
That flung me from my fortune into nothing?
Discharged me his service, shut the doors
Upon my poverty, and scorned my prayers,
Sending me, like a boat without a mast,
To sink or swim? Come, by this hand you die,
I must have life and blood to satisfy
Your father's wrongs.

WIFE. Away, George, away, raise the watch at Ludgate and
bring a mittimus from the justice for this desperate villain.
Now I charge you, gentlemen, see the king's peace kept.
Oh, my heart, what a varlet's this, to offer manslaughter
upon the harmless gentlewoman?

CITIZEN. I warrant thee, sweetheart, we'll have him hampered.

LUCE. Oh, Jasper, be not cruel.
    If thou wilt kill me, smile and do it quickly,
    And let not many deaths appear before me.
    I am a woman made of fear and love,
    A weak, weak woman. Kill not with thy eyes,
    They shoot me through and through. Strike, I am ready;
    And dying, still I love thee.

[*Enter* MERCHANT, HUMPHREY, *and his men.*]

VENTUREWELL.   Whereabouts?

JASPER [*aside*]. No more of this; now to myself again.

HUMPHREY. There, there he stands with sword, like martial
    knight,
    Drawn in his hand. Therefore beware the fight,
    You that are wise, for, were I good Sir Bevis,
    I would not stay his coming, by your leaves.

VENTUREWELL. Sirrah, restore my daughter.

JASPER.   Sirrah, no.

VENTUREWELL. Upon him then.

WIFE. So, down with him, down with him, down with him!
    Cut him i'th' leg, boys, cut him i'th' leg!

VENTUREWELL. Come your ways, minion. I'll provide a
    cage for you, you're grown so tame. Horse her away.

HUMPHREY. Truly I'm glad your forces have the day.

[*Exit all except* JASPER.]

JASPER. They are gone, and I am hurt. My love is lost,
    Never to get again. Oh me unhappy!
    Bleed, bleed, and die. I cannot. Oh my folly,
    Thou hast betrayed me. Hope, where art thou fled?

Tell me if thou be'st anywhere remaining.
Shall I but see my love again? Oh no,
She will not deign to look upon her butcher,
Nor is fit she should. Yet I must venture.
Oh, chance or fortune, or what ere thou art
That men adore for powerful, hear my cry,
And let me loving live, or losing die.

WIFE. Is 'a gone, George?

CITIZEN. Ay, cony.

WIFE. Marry, and let him go, sweetheart, by the faith o' my
body, 'a has put me into such a fright that I tremble, as
they say, as 'twere an aspen leaf. Look a' my little finger,
George, how it shakes. Now, in truth, every member of my
body is the worse for't.

CITIZEN. Come, hug in mine arms, sweet mouse, he shall
not fright thee any more. Alas, mine own dear heart, how
it quivers.

[*Enter* MISTRESS MERRYTHOUGHT, RAFE,
MICHAEL, TIM, HOST, *and a* TAPSTER.]

WIFE. Oh, Rafe, how dost thou, Rafe? How hast thou slept
tonight? Has the knight used thee well?

CITIZEN. Peace, Nell, let Rafe alone.

TAPSTER. Master, the reckoning is not paid.

RAFE. Right courteous knight, who, for the order's sake
Which thou hast ta'en, hang'st out the holy bell,
As I this flaming pestle bear about,
We render thanks to your puissant self,
Your beauteous lady, and your gentle squires,
For thus refreshing of our wearied limbs,
Stiffened with hard achievements in wild desert.

TAPSTER. Sir, there is twelve shillings to pay.

RAFE. Thou merry squire Tapstero, thanks to thee
    For comforting our souls with double jug,
    And if adventurous fortune prick thee forth,
    Thou jovial squire, to follow feats of arms,
    Take heed thou tender every lady's cause,
    Every true knight, and every damsel fair,
    But spill the blood of treacherous saracens
    And false enchanters, that with magic spells
    Have done to death full many a noble knight.

HOST. Thou valiant Knight of the Burning Pestle, give ear
    to me: there is twelve shillings to pay, and as I am a true
    knight, I will not bate a penny.

WIFE. George, I prithee tell me, must Rafe pay twelve
    shillings now?

CITIZEN. No, Nell, no, nothing but the old knight is merry
    with Rafe.

WIFE. Oh, is't nothing else? Rafe will be as merry as he.

RAFE. Sir knight, this mirth of yours becomes you well,
    But to requite this liberal courtesy,
    If any of your squires will follow arms
    He shall receive from my heroic hand
    A knighthood, by the virtue of this pestle.

HOST. Fair knight, I thank you for your noble offer;
    Therefore, gentle knight,
    Twelve shillings you must pay or I must cap you.

WIFE. Look, George, did not I tell thee as much? The
    Knight of the Bell is in earnest, Rafe shall not be
    beholding to him. Give him his money, George, and let
    him go snick up.

CITIZEN. Cap Rafe? No, hold your hand, Sir Knight of the Bell, there's your money. Have you anything to say to Rafe now? Cap Rafe!

WIFE. I would you should know it, Rafe has friends that will not suffer him to be capped for ten times so much, and ten times to the end of that! Now take thy course, Rafe.

MISTRESS MERRYTHOUGHT. Come, Michael, thou and I will go home to thy father. He hath enough left to keep us a day or two, and we'll set fellows abroad to cry our purse and casket. Shall we, Michael?

MICHAEL. Ay, I pray, mother. In truth my foot are full of chilblains with travelling.

WIFE. Faith, and those chilblaines are a foul trouble. Mistress Merrythought, when your youth comes home, let him rub all the soles of his feet and his heels and his ankles with a mouse skin, or if none of your people can catch a mouse, when he goes to bed let him roll his feet in the warm embers, and I warrant you he shall be well; and you may make him put his fingers between his toes and smell to them; it's very sovereign for his head if he be costive.

MISTRESS MERRYTHOUGHT. Master Knight of the Burning Pestle, my son Michael and I bid you farewell. I thank your worship heartily for your kindness.

RAFE. Farewell fair lady, and your tender squire.
If pricking through these deserts I do hear
Of any traitorous knight who, through his guile,
Hath light upon your casket and your purse,
I will despoil him of them and restore them.

MISTRESS MERRYTHOUGHT. I thank your worship.

[*Exit with* MICHAEL.]

RAFE. Dwarf, bear my shield; squire, elevate my lance.
    And now farewell, you Knight of Holy Bell,

CITIZEN. Ay, ay, Rafe, all is paid.

RAFE. But yet before I go, speak, worthy knight,
    If aught you do of sad adventures know,
    Where errant knight may through his prowess win
    Eternal fame and free some gentle souls
    From endless bounds of steel and lingring pain.

HOST [*to* TAPSTER]. Sirrah, go to Nick the barber and bid
    him prepare himself as I told you before, quickly.

TAPSTER. I am gone, sir. [*Exit* TAPSTER.]

HOST. Sir knight, this wilderness affordeth none
    But the great venture, where full many a knight
    Hath tried his prowess and come off with shame,
    And where I would not have you lose your life
    Against no man, but furious fiend of hell.

RAFE. Speak on, sir knight, tell what he is and where:
    For here I vow upon my blazing badge
    Never to blaze a day in quietness,
    But bread and water will I only eat,
    And the green herb and rock shall be my couch,
    Till I have quelled that man or beast or fiend
    That works such damage to all errant knights.

HOST. Not far from hence, near a craggy cliff
    At the north end of this distressed town,
    There doth stand a lowly house,
    Ruggedly builded, and in it a cave
    In which an ugly giant now doth won,
    Ycleped Barbaroso. In his hand
    He shakes a naked lance of purest steel,
    With sleeves turned up, and him before he wears

A motley garment to preserve his clothes
From blood of those knights which he massacres,
And ladies gentle. Without his door doth hang
A copper basin on a prickant spear,
At which, no sooner gentle knights can knock,
But the shrill sound fierce Barbaroso hears,
And rushing forth, brings in the errant knight
And sets him down in an enchanted chair.
Then, with an engine which he hath prepared
With forty teeth, he claws his courtly crown,
Next makes him wink, and underneath his chin
He plants a brazen piece of mighty board
And knocks his bullets round about his cheeks,
Whilst with his fingers and an instrument
With which he snaps his hair off, he doth fill
The wretch's ears with a most hideous noise.
Thus every knight adventurer he doth trim,
And now no creature dares encounter him.

RAFE. In God's name, I will fight with him. Kind sir,
Go but before me to this dismal cave
Where this huge giant Barbaroso dwells,
And by that virtue that brave Rosicleer
That damned brood of ugly giants slew,
And Palmerin Frannarco overthrew,
I doubt not but to curb this traitor foul,
And to the devil send his guilty soul.

HOST. Brave sprighted knight, thus far I will perform
This, your request: I'll bring you within sight
Of this most loathsome place, inhabited
By a more loathsome man, but dare not stay,
For his main force swoops all he sees away.

RAFE. Saint George, set on before! March, squire and page.

[*Exit.*]

WIFE. George, dost think Rafe will confound the giant?

CITIZEN. I hold my cap to a farthing he does. Why, Nell, I saw him wrestle with the great Dutchman and hurl him.

WIFE. Faith, and that Dutchman was a goodly man, if all things were answerable to his bigness. And yet they say there was a Scottish man higher than he, and that they two and a knight met and saw one another for nothing. But of all the sights that ever were in London since I was married, methinks the little child that was so fair grown about the members was the prettiest, that and the hermaphrodite.

CITIZEN. Nay, by your leave, Nell, Ninivie was better.

WIFE. Ninivie? Oh, that was the story of Joan and the Wall, was it not, George?

CITIZEN. Yes, lamb.

[*Enter* MISTRESS MERRYTHOUGHT.]

WIFE. Look, George, here comes Mistress Merrythought again, and I would have Rafe come and fight with the giant. I tell you true, I long to see't.

CITIZEN. Good Mistress Merrythought, begone, I pray you for my sake. I pray you forbear a little. You shall have audience presently. I have a little business.

WIFE. Mistress Merrythought, if it please you to refrain your passion a little till Rafe have dispatched the giant out of the way, we shall think ourselves much bound to thank you. I thank you, good Mistress Merrythought.

[*Exit* MISTRESS MERRYTHOUGHT.]

[*Enter a* BOY.]

CITIZEN. Boy, come hither. Send away Rafe and this
whoreson giant quickly.

BOY. In good faith, sir, we cannot. You'll utterly spoil our
play, and make it to be hissed, and it cost money. You will
not suffer us to go on with our plots. I pray, gentlemen,
rule him.

CITIZEN. Let him come now and dispatch this and I'll
trouble you no more.

BOY. Will you give me your hand of that?

WIFE. Give him thy hand, George, do, and I'll kiss him. I
warrant thee the youth means plainly.

BOY. I'll send him to you presently.

[*Exit* BOY.]

WIFE. I thank you, little youth. Faith, the child hath a sweet
breath, George, but I think it be troubled with the worms.
Carduus benedictus and mare's milk were the only thing in
the world for't. Oh, Rafe's here, George. God send thee
good luck, Rafe.

[*Enter* RAFE, HOST, TIM *and* GEORGE.]

HOST. Puissant knight, yonder his mansion is –
Lo, where the spear and copper basin are.
Behold the string on which hangs many a tooth
Drawn from the gentle jaw of wand'ring knights.
I dare not stay to sound, he will appear.

[*Exit* HOST.]

RAFE. Oh, faint not heart. Susan, my lady dear,
The cobbler's maid in Milk Street, for whose sake
I take these arms; oh, let the thought of thee

Carry thy knight through all adventurous deeds,
And in the honor of thy beauteous self
May I destroy this monster Barbaroso.
Knock, squire, upon the basin till it break
With the shrill strokes, or till the giant speak.

[*Enter* BARBER.]

WIFE. Oh George, the giant, the giant! Now, Rafe, for thy
life!

BARBER. What fond unknowing wight is this, that dares
So rudely knock at Barbaroso's cell,
Where no man comes but leaves his fleece behind?

RAFE. I, traitorous caitiff, who am sent by fate
To punish all the sad enormities
Thou hast committed against ladies gentle
And errant knights. Traitor to God and men,
Prepare thyself. This is the dismal hour
Appointed for thee to give strict account
Of all thy beastly, treacherous villainies.

BARBER. Foolhardy knight, full soon thou shalt aby
This fond reproach, thy body will I bang,
[*Takes down his pole.*]
And lo, upon that string thy teeth shall hang.
Prepare thyself, for dead soon shalt thou be.

RAFE. Saint George for me!

BARBER. Gargantua for me.

[*They fight.*]

WIFE. To him, Rafe, to him! Hold up the giant! Set out thy
leg before, Rafe!

CITIZEN. Falsify a blow, Rafe, falsify a blow! The giant lies
　　open on the left side!

WIFE. Bear't off, bear't off still! There, boy – Oh, Rafe's
　　almost down, Rafe's almost down!

RAFE. Susan, inspire me! Now have up again.

WIFE. Up, up, up, up, up! So, Rafe, down with him, down
　　with him, Rafe.

CITIZEN. Fetch him over the hip, boy.

WIFE. There, boy, kill, kill, kill, kill, kill, Rafe!

CITIZEN. No, Rafe, get all out of him first.

　　[RAFE *knocks the* BARBER *down.*]

RAFE. Presumptuous man, see to what desperate end
　　Thy treachery hath brought thee. The just gods,
　　Who never prosper those that do despise them,
　　For all the villainies which thou hast done
　　To knights and ladies now have paid thee home
　　By my stiff arm, a knight adventurous.
　　But say, vile wretch, before I send thy soul
　　To sad Avernus, whither it must go,
　　What captives holdst thou in thy sable cave?

BARBER. Go in and free them all, thou hast the day.

RAFE. Go, squire and dwarf, search in this dreadful cave,
　　And free the wretched prisoners from their bonds.

　　[*Exit* TIM *and* GEORGE.]

BARBER. I crave for mercy, as thou art a knight
　　And scorn'st to spill the blood of those that beg.

RAFE. Thou showed'st no mercy nor shalt thou have any.
　　Prepare thyself, for thou shalt surely die.

[*Enter* TIM *leading one winking, with a basin under his chin.*]

TIM. Behold, brave knight, here is one prisoner
    Whom this wild man hath used as you see.

WIFE. This is the wisest word I hear the squire speak.

RAFE. Speak what thou art, and how thou hast been used,
    That I may give him condign punishment.

1st KNIGHT. I am a knight that took my journey post
    Northward from London, and in courteous wise
    This giant trained me to his den
    Under pretence of killing of the itch,
    And all my body with a powder strewed,
    That smarts and stings, and cut away my beard
    And my curled locks wherein were ribbons tied,
    And with a water washed my tender eyes,
    Whilst up and down about me still he skipped,
    Whose virtue is that till my eyes be wiped
    With a dry cloth, for this my soul disgrace,
    I shall not dare to look a dog i'th' face.

WIFE. Alas, poor knight. Relieve him, Rafe, relieve poor
    knights whilst you live.

RAFE. My trusty squire, convey him to the town,
    Where he may find relief. Adieu, fair knight.

    [*Exit* KNIGHT.]

    [*Enter* GEORGE, *leading one with a patch over his nose.*]

GEORGE. Puissant Knight of the Burning Pestle hight,
    See here another wretch, whom this foul beast
    Hath scorched and scored in this inhuman wise.

RAFE. Speak me thy name, and eke thy place of birth,
    And what hath been thy usage in this cave.

2nd KNIGHT. I am a knight, Sir Pockhole is my name,
    And by my birth I am a Londoner,
    Free by my copy, but my ancestors
    Were Frenchmen all. And riding hard this way
    Upon a trotting horse, my bones did ache,
    And I, faint knight, to ease my weary limbs,
    Light at this cave, when straight this furious fiend,
    With sharpest instrument of purest steel,
    Did cut the gristle of my nose away,
    And in the place this velvet plaster stands.
    Relieve me, gentle knight, out of his hands.

WIFE. Good Rafe, relieve Sir Pockhole and send him away,
    for, in truth, his breath stinks.

RAFE. Convey him straight after the other knight.
    Sir Pockhole, fare you well.

2nd KNIGHT.   Kind sir, goodnight.

    [*Exit.*]

    [*Cries within.*]

3rd KNIGHT [*within*]. Deliver us!

WOMAN [*within*]. Deliver us!

WIFE. Hark, George, what a woeful cry there is. I think
    some woman lies in there.

3rd KNIGHT [*within*]. Deliver us!

WOMAN [*within*]. Deliver us!

RAFE. What ghastly noise is this? Speak, Barbaroso
    Or by this blazing steel thy head goes off.

BARBER. Prisoners of mine, whom I in diet keep.
    Send lower down into the cave,

And in a tub that's heated smoking hot,
There may they find them and deliver them.

RAFE. Run, squire and dwarf, deliver them with speed.

[*Exit* TIM *and* GEORGE.]

WIFE. But will not, Rafe, kill this giant, surely? I am afraid if
he let him go he will do as much hurt as ever he did.

CITIZEN. Not so, mouse, neither, if he could convert him.

WIFE. Ay, George, if he could convert him, but a giant is not
so soon converted as one of us ordinary people. There's a
pretty tale of a witch that had the devil's mark about her,
God bless us, that had a giant to her son, that was called
Lob-lie-by-the-fire. Didst never hear it, George?

[*Enter* TIM *leading a man with a glass of lotion in his hand, and*
GEORGE *leading a woman with diet-bread and drink.*]

CITIZEN. Peace, Nell, here comes the prisoners.

GEORGE. Here be these pinèd wretches, manful knight,
That for this six weeks have not seen a wight.

RAFE. Deliver what you are and how you came
To this sad cave, and what your usage was?

3rd KNIGHT. I am an errant knight that followed arms
With spear and shield, and in my tender years
I strucken was with Cupid's fiery shaft
And fell in love with this my lady dear,
And stole her from her friends in Turnbull Street,
And bore her up and down from town to town,
Where we did eat and drink and music hear,
Till at the length at this unhappy town
We did arrive, and, coming to this cave,
This beast us caught and put us in a tub,

Where we this two months sweat, and should have done
Another month if you had not relieved us.

WOMAN. This bread and water hath our diet been,
Together with a rib cut from a neck
Of burned mutton; hard hath been our fare.
Release us from this ugly giant's snare.

3rd KNIGHT. This hath been half the food we have
received,
But only twice a day, for novelty,
He gave a spoonful of his hearty broth
[*He pulls out a syringe.*]
To each of us, through this same slender quill.

RAFE. From this infernal monster you shall go,
That useth knights and gentle ladies so.
Convey them hence.

[*Exit* 3RD KNIGHT *and* WOMAN.]

CITIZEN. Cony, I can tell thee the gentlemen like Rafe.

WIFE. Ay, George, I see it well enough. Gentlemen, I thank
you all heartily for gracing my man Raph, and I promise
you, you shall see him oft'ner.

BARBER. Mercy, great knight, I do recant my ill,
And henceforth never gentle blood will spill.

RAFE. I give thee mercy, but yet thou shalt swear
Upon my burning pestle to perform
Thy promise uttered.

BARBER. I swear and kiss.

RAFE. Depart then and amend.
[*Exit* BARBER.]
Come, squire and dwarf, the sun grows towards his set,
And we have many more adventures yet.

[*Exit.*]

CITIZEN. Now Raph is in this humor, I know he would ha'
    beaten all the boys in the house if they had been set on
    him.

WIFE. Ay, George, but it is well as it is. I warrant you the
    gentlemen do consider what it is to overthrow a giant. But
    look, George, here comes Mistress Merrythought and her
    son Michael. Now you are welcome, Mistress
    Merrythought, now Raph has done, you may go on.

[*Enter* MISTRESS MERRYTHOUGHT *and* MICHAEL.]

MISTRESS MERRYTHOUGHT. Mick, my boy?

MICHAEL. Ay, forsooth, Mother.

MISTRESS MERRYTHOUGHT. Be merry, Mick, we are at
    home now, where, I warrant you, yon shall find the house
    slung out of the windows.
    [*Music from within.*]
    Hark, hey dogs, hey, this is the old world, i'faith, with my
    husband. I'll get in among them, I'll play them such a
    lesson that they shall have little list to come scraping hither
    again. Why, Master Merrythought, husband, Charles
    Merrythought!

OLD MERRYTHOUGHT [*sings, within*].
    If you will sing, and dance, and laugh,
    And hollo and laugh again,
    And then cry, 'There, boys, there', why then,
    One, two, three, and four,
    We shall be merry within this hour.

MISTRESS MERRYTHOUGHT. Why, Charles, do you not
    know your own natural wife? I say, open the door and
    turn me out those mangy companions – 'tis more than

time that they were fellow like with you. You are a
gentleman, Charles, and an old man and father of two
children, and I myself, though I say it, by my mother's side
niece to a worshipful gentleman, and a conductor. He has
been three times in His Majesty's service at Chester, and is
now the fourth time, God bless him and his charge upon
his journey.

OLD MERRYTHOUGHT [*sings, within*].
  Go from my window, love, go,
  Go from my window, my dear,
  The wind and the rain
  Will drive you back again,
  You cannot be lodged here.
Hark you, Mistress Merrythought, you that walk upon
adventures and forsake your husband because he sings with
never a penny in his purse. What, shall I think myself the
worse? Faith, no, I'll be merry. You come not here, here's
none but lads of mettle, lives of a hundred years and
upwards. Care never drunk their bloods, nor want made
them warble. [*Sings.*]
  Heigh-ho, my heart is heavy.

MISTRESS MERRYTHOUGHT. Why, Master
Merrythought, what am I that you should laugh me to
scorn thus abruptly? Am I not your fellow-feeler, as we
may say, in all our miseries? Your comforter in health and
sickness? Have I not brought you children? Are they not
like you, Charles? Look upon thine own image, hard-
hearted man. And yet for all this –

OLD MERRYTHOUGHT [*sings, within*].
  Begone, begone, my juggy, my puggy,
  Begone my love, my dear.
  The weather is warm,
  'Twill do thee no harm,

Thou canst not be lodged here.
Be merry, boys. Some light music, and more wine.

WIFE. He's not in earnest, I hope, George, is he?

CITIZEN. What if he be, sweetheart?

WIFE. Marry, if he be George, I'll make bold to tell him he's an ingrant old man to use his bed-fellow so scurvily.

CITIZEN. What, how does he use her, honey?

WIFE. Marry come up, Sir Sauce-box, I think you'll take his part, will you not? Lord, how hot are you grown! You are a fine man, an you had a fine dog: it becomes you sweetly.

CITIZEN. Nay, prithee, Nell, chide not, for as I am an honest man and a true Christian grocer, I do not like his doings.

WIFE. I cry you mercy then, George. You know we are all frail and full of infirmities. D'ee hear, Master Merrythought, may I crave a word with you?

OLD MERRYTHOUGHT [*within*].
Strike up lively lads.

WIFE. I had not thought in truth, Master Merrythought, that a man of your age and discretion, as I may say, being a gentleman and therefore known by your gentle conditions, could have used so little respect to the weakness of his wife. For your wife is your own flesh, the staff of your age, your yoke-fellow, with whose help you draw through the mire of this transitory world. Nay, she's your own rib. And again –

OLD MERRYTHOUGHT [*sings, within*].
I come not hither for thee to teach,
I have no pulpit for thee to preach,

I would thou hadst kissed me under the breech,
As thou art a lady gay.

WIFE. Marry, with a vengeance! I am heartily sorry for the
poor gentlewoman. But if I were thy wife, i'faith grey-
beard, i'faith –

CITIZEN. I prithee, sweet honeysuckle, be content.

WIFE. Give me such words that am a gentlewoman born.
Hang him, hoary rascal! Get me some drink, George, I am
almost molten with fretting. Now beshrew his knave's heart
for it.

OLD MERRYTHOUGHT. Play me a light Lavalto. Come,
be frolic, fill the good fellows' wine.

MISTRESS MERRYTHOUGHT. Why Master
Merrythought, are you disposed to make me wait here?
You'll open, I hope? I'll fetch them that shall open, else.

OLD MERRYTHOUGHT. Good woman, if you will sing I'll
give you something. If not – [*Sings.*]
You are no love for me, Margaret,
I am no love for you.
Come aloft, boys, aloft.

MISTRESS MERRYTHOUGHT. Now a churl's fart in your
teeth, sir. Come, Mick, we'll not trouble him. 'A shall not
ding us i'th' teeth with his bread and his broth, that he
shall not. Come, boy, I'll provide for thee, I warrant thee.
We'll go to Master Venturewell's, the Merchant. I'll get his
letter to mine host of the Bell in Waltham – there I'll place
thee with the tapster. Will not that do well for thee, Mick?
And let me alone for that old cuckoldly knave, your father.
I'll use him in his kind, I warrant ye.

[*Exit.*]

[Interlude]

[*Music*.]

[*Enter* BOY.]

WIFE. Come, George, where's the beer?

CITIZEN. Here, love.

WIFE. This old fornicating fellow will not out of my mind
    yet. Gentlemen, I'll begin to you all, I desire more of your
    acquaintance, with all my heart. [*Drinks*.] Fill the
    gentlemen some beer, George.

[*The* BOY *dances*.]

WIFE. Look, George, the little boy's come again. Methinks he
    looks something like the Prince of Orange in his long
    stocking, if he had a little harness about his neck. George,
    I will have him dance 'Fading'. 'Fading' is a fine jig, I'll
    assure you, Gentlemen. Begin, brother. Now 'a capers,
    sweetheart, now a turn a th'toe, and then tumble. Cannot
    you tumble, youth?

BOY. No, indeed, forsooth.

WIFE. Nor eat fire?

BOY. Neither.

WIFE. Why then, I thank you heartily. There's twopence to
    buy you points withall.

ACT IV

Enter JASPER *and* BOY.

JASPER [*gives him a letter*].
    There boy, deliver this: but do it well.
    Hast thou provided me four lusty fellows?
    Able to carry me? And art thou perfect
    In all thy business?

BOY.   Sir, you need not fear.
    I have my lesson here and cannot miss it.
    The men are ready for you, and what else
    Pertains to this employment.

JASPER [*gives him money*]. There my boy,
    Take it, but buy no land.

BOY.   Faith, sir, 'twere rare
    To see so young a purchaser. I fly,
    And on my wings carry your destiny.

    [*Exit.*]

JASPER. Go and be happy. Now, my latest hope
    Forsake me not, but fling thy anchor out
    And let it hold. Stand fixed, thou rolling stone,
    Till I enjoy my dearest. Hear me, all
    You powers that rule in men celestial.

    [*Exit.*]

WIFE. Go thy ways, thou art as crooked a sprig as ever grew
    in London. I warrant him he'll come to some naughty end

or other, for his looks say no less. Besides, his father, you
know, George, is none of the best. You heard him take me
up like a flirt-gill and sing bawdy songs upon me. But,
i'faith, if I live, George –

CITIZEN. Let me alone, sweetheart. I have a trick in my
head shall lodge him in the arches for one year and make
him sing *peccavi* ere I leave him, and yet he shall never
know who hurt him neither.

WIFE. Do, my good George, do.

CITIZEN. What shall we have Rafe do now, boy?

BOY. You shall have what you will, sir.

CITIZEN. Why, so, sir, go and fetch me him then, and let
the Sophy of Persia come and christen him a child.

BOY. Believe me, sir, that will not do so well. 'Tis stale. It
has been had before at the Red Bull.

WIFE. George, let Rafe travel over great hills, and let him be
weary and come to the King of Cracovia's house, covered
with velvet, and there let the King's daughter stand in her
window all in beaten gold, combing her golden locks with
a comb of ivory, and let her spy Rafe and fall in love with
him, and come down to him, and carry him into her
father's house, and then let Rafe talk with her.

CITIZEN. Well said, Nell, it shall be so. Boy, let's ha't done
quickly.

BOY. Sir, if you will imagine all this to be done already, you
shall hear them talk together. But we cannot present a
house covered with black velvet and a lady in beaten gold.

CITIZEN. Sir, boy, let's ha't as you can, then.

BOY. Besides, it will show ill-favouredly to have a grocer's
prentice to court a king's daughter.

CITIZEN. Will it so, sir? You are well read in histories! I
pray you, what was Sir Dagonet? Was not he prentice to a
grocer in London? Read the play of *The Four Prentices of
London*, where they toss their pikes so. I pray you, fetch
him in, sir, fetch him in.

BOY. It shall be done – it is not our fault, gentlemen.

[*Exit.*]

WIFE. Now we shall see fine doings, I warrant thee, George.
Oh, here they come! How prettily the King of Cracovia's
daughter is dressed.

[*Enter* RAFE *and the* LADY, TIM *and* GEORGE.]

CITIZEN. Ay, Nell, it is the fashion of that country, I warrant
thee.

LADY. Welcome, sir knight, unto my father's court.
King of Moldavia; unto me Pompiona,
His daughter dear. But sure you do not like
Your entertainment, that will stay with us
No longer but a night.

RAFE.   Damsel right fair,
I am on many sad adventures bound,
That call me forth into the wilderness.
Besides, my horse's back is something galled,
Which will enforce me ride a sober pace.
But many thanks, fair lady, be to you,
For using errant knight with courtesy.

LADY. But say, brave knight, what is your name and birth?

RAFE. My name is Rafe. I am an Englishman,
    As true as steel, a hearty Englishman,
    And prentice to a grocer in the Strand,
    By deed indent, of which I have one part.
    But fortune calling me to follow arms,
    On me this holy order I did take
    Of Burning Pestle, which in all men's eyes
    I bear, confounding ladies' enemies.

LADY. Oft have I heard of your brave countrymen
    And fertile soil, and store of wholesome food.
    My father oft will tell me of a drink
    In England found, and 'nipitato' called,
    Which driveth all the sorrow from your hearts.

RAFE. Lady 'tis true, you need not lay your lips
    To better nipitato than there is.

LADY. And of a wild fowl he will often speak,
    Which 'powdered beef and mustard' called is.
    For there have been great wars 'twixt us and you.
    But truly, Rafe, it was not long of me.
    Tell me then, Rafe, could you contented be
    To wear a lady's favour in your shield?

RAFE. I am a knight of religious order
    And will not wear a favour of a lady's
    That trusts in Antichrist and false traditions.

CITIZEN. Well said, Rafe, convert her if thou canst.

RAFE. Besides, I have a lady of my own
    In merry England, for whose virtuous sake
    I took these arms, and Susan is her name,
    A cobbler's maid in Milk Street, whom I vow
    Ne'er to forsake whilst life and pestle last.

LADY. Happy that cobbling dame, who'er she be,
    That for her own, dear Rafe, hath gotten thee.
    Unhappy I that ne'er shall see the day
    To see thee more, that bear'st my heart away.

RAFE. Lady farewell, I must needs take my leave.

LADY. Hard-hearted Rafe, that ladies dost deceive.

CITIZEN. Hark thee, Rafe, there's money for thee. Give
    something in the King of Cracovia's house, be not
    beholding to him.

RAFE. Lady, before I go, I must remember
    Your father's officers, who, truth to tell,
    Have been about me very diligent.
    Hold up thy snowy hand, thou princely maid:
    There's twelve pence for your father's chamberlain
    And another shilling for his cook,
    For, by my troth, the goose was roasted well;
    And twelve pence for your father's horse-keeper
    For 'nointing my horse back, and for his butter
    There is another shilling; to the maid
    That washed my boot-hose, there's an English groat;
    And twopence to the boy that wiped my boots.
    And last, fair Lady, there is for your self
    Threepence to buy you pins at Bumbo Fair.

LADY. Full many thanks, and I will keep them safe
    Till all the heads be off, for thy sake, Rafe.

RAFE. Advance my squire and dwarf, I cannot stay.

LADY. Thou kill'st my heart in parting thus away.

    [*Exit.*]

WIFE. I commend Rafe, yet that he will not stoop to a
    Cracovian. There's properer women in London than any

are there, iwis. But here comes Master Humphrey and his
love again now, George.

CITIZEN. Ay, cony, peace.

[*Enter* VENTUREWELL, HUMPHREY, LUCE, *and* BOY.]

VENTUREWELL. Go, get you up, I will not be entreated.
And, gossip mine, I'll keep you sure hereafter
From gadding out again with boys and unthrifts.
Come, they are women's tears, I know your fashion.
Go, sirrah, lock her in and keep the key
Safe as your life.

[*Exit* LUCE *and* BOY.]

            Now, my son Humphrey,
You may both rest assured of my love
In this and reap your own desire.

HUMPHREY.
I see this love you speak of through your daughter,
Although the hole be little, and hereafter
Will yield the like in all I may or can,
Fitting a Christian and a gentleman.

VENTUREWELL.
I do believe you, my good son, and thank you,
For 'twere an impudence to think you flattered.

HUMPHREY. It were indeed, but shall I tell you why?
I have been beaten twice about the lie.

VENTUREWELL. Well, son, no more of compliment. My
daughter
Is yours again. Appoint the time and take her –
We'll have no stealing for it. I myself
And some few of our friends will see you married.

HUMPHREY. I would you would, i'faith, for be it known
   I ever was afraid to lie alone.

VENTUREWELL. Some three days hence, then.

HUMPHREY.   Three days, let me see;
   'Tis somewhat of the most, yet I agree
   Because I mean against the pointed day,
   To visit all my friends in new array.

   [*Enter* SERVANT.]

SERVANT. Sir, there's a gentlewoman without would speak
   with your worship.

VENTUREWELL. What is she?

SERVANT. Sir, I asked her not.

VENTUREWELL. Bid her come in.

   [*Exit* SERVANT.]

   [*Enter* MISTRESS MERRYTHOUGHT *and* MICHAEL.]

MISTRESS MERRYTHOUGHT. Peace be to your worship,
   I come as a poor suitor to you, sir, in the behalf of this
   child.

VENTUREWELL. Are you not wife to Merrythought?

MISTRESS MERRYTHOUGHT. Yes, truly, would I had
   ne'er seen his eyes! He has undone me and himself, and
   his children, and there he lives at home and sings, and
   hoits, and revels among his drunken companions. But I
   warrant you, where to get a penny to put bread in his
   mouth he knows not: And therefore, if it like your worship,
   I would entreat your letter to the honest host of the Bell in
   Waltham, that I may place my child under the protection
   of his tapster, in some settled course of life.

VENTUREWELL. I'm glad the heavens have heard my
prayers. Thy husband,
When I was ripe in sorrows, laughed at me.
Thy son, like an unthankful wretch, I having
Redeemed him from his fall and made him mine,
To show his love again, first stole my daughter,
Then wronged this gentleman, and, last of all,
Gave me that grief had almost brought me down
Unto my grave, had not a stronger hand
Relieved my sorrows. Go, and weep as I did,
And be unpitied, for here I profess
An everlasting hate to all thy name.

MISTRESS MERRYTHOUGHT. Will you so, sir? How say
you by that? Come, Mick, let him keep his wind to cool
his pottage. We'll go to thy nurse's, Mick. She knits silk
stockings, boy, and we'll knit too, boy, and be beholding to
none of them all.

[*Exit* MICHAEL *and* MOTHER.]

[*Enter a* BOY *with a letter.*]

BOY. Sir, I take it you are the master of this house.

VENTUREWELL. How then, boy?

BOY. Then to yourself, sir, comes this letter.

VENTUREWELL. From whom, my pretty boy?

BOY. From him that was your servant – but no more
Shall that name ever be, for he is dead.
Grief of your purchased anger broke his heart.
I saw him die and from his hand received
This paper with a charge to bring it hither.
Read it and satisfy yourself in all.

VENTUREWELL [*reads*]. 'Sir, that I have wronged your love,
 I must confess, in which I have purchased to myself,
 besides mine own undoing, the ill opinion of my friends.
 Let not your anger, good sir, outlive me, but suffer me to
 rest in peace with your forgiveness. Let my body, if a dying
 man may so much prevail with you, be brought to your
 daughter that she may know my hot flames are now
 buried, and, withall, receive a testimony of the zeal I bore
 her virtue. Farewell for ever, and be ever happy. Jasper.'
 God's hand is great in this. I do forgive him.
 Yet am I glad he's quiet, where I hope
 He will not bite again. Boy, bring the body
 And let him have his will, if that be all.

BOY. 'Tis here without, sir.

VENTUREWELL.   So, sir, if you please
 You may conduct it in, I do not fear it.

HUMPHREY. I'll be your usher, boy, for though I say it,
 He owed me something once and well did pay it.

 [*Exit.*]

 [*Enter* LUCE *alone.*]

LUCE. If there be any punishment inflicted
 Upon the miserable more than yet I feel,
 Let it together seize me, and at once
 Press down my soul. I cannot bear the pain
 Of these delaying tortures. Thou that art
 The end of all and the sweet rest of all,
 Come, come, oh Death, bring me to thy peace,
 And blot out all the memory I nourish
 Both of my father and my cruel friend.
 Oh wretched maid, still living to be wretched,
 To be a say to Fortune in her changes

And grow to number times and woes together.
How happy had I been if, being born,
My grave had been my cradle?

[*Enter* SERVANT.]

SERVANT.   By your leave
Young mistress, here's a boy hath brought a coffin.
What a would say I know not, but your father
Charged me to give you notice. Here they come.

[*Enter* BOY *and another bearing a coffin,* JASPER *in it.*]

LUCE. For me I hope 'tis come, and 'tis most welcome.

BOY. Fair mistress, let me not add greater grief
To that great store you have already. Jasper,
That whilst he lived was yours, now dead,
And here enclosed, commanded me to bring
His body hither, and to crave a tear
From those fair eyes, though he deserve not pity,
To deck his funeral: for so he bid me
Tell her for whom he died.

LUCE.   He shall have many.
Good friends depart a little, whilst I take
My leave of this dead man, that once I loved.

[*Exit* BOY *and* COFFIN-CARRIER.]

Hold yet a little, life, and then I give thee
To thy first heavenly being. Oh, my friend!
Hast thou deceived me thus, and got before me?
I shall not long be after, but believe me,
Thou wert too cruel, Jasper, 'gainst thyself,
In punishing the fault I could have pardoned,
With so untimely death. Thou didst not wrong me
But ever wert most kind, most true, most loving

And I the most unkind, most false, most cruel.
Didst thou but ask a tear? I'll give thee all,
Even all my eyes can pour down, all my sighs
And all myself, before thou goest from me.
There are but sparing rites, but if thy soul
Be yet about this place and can behold
And see what I prepare to deck thee with,
It shall go up, borne on the wings of peace,
And satisfied. First will I sing thy dirge,
Then kiss thy pale lips, and then die myself,
And fill one coffin and one grave together.

Song.
Come you whose loves are dead,
And whilst I sing,
Weep and wring
Every hand and every bead,
Bind with cypress and sad yew,
Ribbons black, and candles blue,
For him that was of men most true.
Come with heavy mourning,
And on his grave
Let him have
Sacrifice of sighs and groaning,
Let him have fair flowers enow,
White and purple, green and yellow,
For him that was of men most true.
Thou sable cloth, sad cover of my joys,
I lift thee up and thus I meet with death.

JASPER [*rising from the coffin*].
And thus you meet the living.

LUCE.   Save me, heaven!

JASPER. Nay, do not fly me, fair, I am no spirit.
Look better on me. Do you know me yet?

LUCE. Oh, thou dear shadow of my friend.

JASPER.   Dear substance,
    I swear I am no shadow; feel my hand,
    It is the same it was. I am your Jasper,
    Your Jasper that's yet living, and yet loving.
    Pardon my rash attempt, my foolish proof
    I put in practice of your constancy,
    For sooner should my sword have drunk my blood,
    And set my soul at liberty, than drawn
    The least drop from that body, for which boldness
    Doom me to any thing: if death, I take it,
    And willingly.

LUCE.   This death I'll give you for it.

[*Kisses him.*]

    So, now I am satisfied: you are no spirit,
    But my own truest, truest, truest, friend,
    Why do you come thus to me?

JASPER.   First, to see you,
    Then to convey you hence.

LUCE.   It cannot be,
    For I am locked up here, and watched at all hours,
    That 'tis impossible for me to 'scape.

JASPER. Nothing more possible. Within this coffin
    Do you convey yourself; let me alone,
    I have the wits of twenty men about me.
    Only I crave the shelter of your closet
    A little, and then fear me not. Creep in,
    That they may presently convey you hence.
    Fear nothing, dearest love, I'll be your second

[LUCE *lies in the coffin and* JASPER *covers her with a cloth.*]

    Lie close, so, all goes well yet. Boy!

[*Enter* BOY *and* COFFIN-CARRIER.]

BOY. At hand, sir.

JASPER. Convey away the coffin, and be wary.

BOY. 'Tis done already.

JASPER. Now must I go conjure.

[*Exit*.]

[*Enter* VENTUREWELL.]

VENTUREWELL. Boy, boy!

BOY. Your servant, sir.

VENTUREWELL. Do me this kindness boy – hold, here's a crown: before thou bury the body of this fellow, carry it to his old merry father, and salute him from me, and bid him sing; he hath cause.

BOY. I will, sir.

VENTUREWELL. And then bring me word what tune he is in, and have another crown. But do it truly. I have fitted him a bargain now will vex him.

BOY. God bless your worship's health, sir.

VENTUREWELL. Farewell, boy.

[*Exit*.]

[*Enter* MASTER MERRYTHOUGHT.]

WIFE. Ah, old Merrythought, art thou there again? Let's hear some of thy songs.

OLD MERRYTHOUGHT [*sings*].
Who can sing a merrier note
Thou he that cannot change a great?

Not a denier left and yet my heart leaps. I do wonder yet, as old as I am, that any man will follow a trade, or serve, that may sing and laugh and walk the streets. My wife and both my sons are I know not where, I have nothing left, nor know I how to come by meat to supper, yet am I merry still, for I know I shall find it upon the table at six o'clock. Therefore hang thought. [*Sings.*]

I would not be a serving man
To carry the cloak-bag still,
Nor would I be a falconer
The greedy hawks to fill.
But I would be in a good house,
And have a good master, too,
But I would eat and drink of the best,
And no work would I do.

This is that keeps life and soul together: mirth. This is the Philosopher's Stone that they write so much on, that keeps a man ever young.

[*Enter a* BOY.]

BOY. Sir, they say they know all your money is gone and they will trust you for no more drink.

OLD MERRYTHOUGHT. Will they not? Let 'em choose. The best is, I have mirth at home and need not send abroad for that. Let them keep their drink to themselves. [*Sings.*] *For Jillian of Bury she dwells on a hill,*
And she hath good beer and ale to sell,
And of good fellows she thinks no ill.
And thither will we go now, now, now,
And thither will we go now.
And when you have made a little stay,
You need not ask what is to pay,
But kiss your hostess and go your way.
And thither, &c.

[*Enter another* BOY.]

2nd BOY. Sir, I can get no bread for supper.

OLD MERRYTHOUGHT. Hang bread and supper. Let's
preserve our mirth and we shall never feel hunger, I'll
warrant you. Let's have a catch. Boy, follow me, come sing
this catch. [*They sing.*]
Ho, ho, no body at home,
Meat, nor drink, nor money ha' we none,
Fill the pot, Eedy,
Never more need I.
So, boys, enough. Follow me. Let's change our place and
we shall laugh afresh.

[*Exit.*]

[Interlude]

WIFE. Let him go, George. 'A shall not have any
countenance from us, not a good word from any i'th'
company, if I may strike stroke in't.

CITIZEN. No more, 'a sha'not love. But, Nell, I will have
Rafe do a very notable matter now, to the eternal honour
and glory of all grocers. Sirrah! You there, boy! Can none
of you hear?

BOY. Sir, your pleasure.

CITIZEN. Let Rafe come out on May Day in the morning
and speak upon a conduit with all his scarfs about him,
and his feathers, and his rings and his knacks.

BOY. Why, sir, you do not think of our plot. What will
become of that, then?

CITIZEN. Why, sir, I care not what become on't. I'll have
him come out or I'll fetch him out myself. I'll have
something done in honour of the city. Besides, he hath
been long enough upon adventures. Bring him out quickly,
for, if I come amongst you –

BOY. Well, sir, he shall come out. But if our play miscarry,
sir, you are like to pay for't.

[*Exit.*]

CITIZEN. Bring him away, then.

WIFE. This will be brave, i'faith. George, shall not he dance
the morris too, for the credit of the Strand?

CITIZEN. No, sweetheart, it will be too much for the boy.
Oh, there he is, Nell. He's reasonable well in reparel, but
he has not rings enough.

[*Enter* RAFE.]

RAFE. London, to thee I do present the merry month of May.
Let each true subject be content to hear me what I say,
For, from the top of conduit head, as plainly may appear,
I will both tell my name to you and wherefore I came here.
My name is Rafe, by due descent, though not ignoble I,
Yet far inferior to the flock of gracious grocery.
And by the common counsel of my fellows in the Strand,
With gilded staff, and crossed scarf, the May Lord here
    I stand.
Rejoice, oh English hearts, rejoice. Rejoice, oh lovers dear.
Rejoice, oh city, town and country. Rejoice eke every shire.
For now the flagrant flowers do spring and sprout in
    seemly sort,

The little birds do sit and sing, the lambs do make fine sport.
And now the birchen tree doth bud, that makes the
    schoolboy cry,
The morris rings while hobby-horse doth foot it feateously.
The lords and ladies now abroad for their disport and play,
Do kiss sometimes upon the grass, and sometimes in the hay.
Now butter with a leaf of sage is good to purge the blood,
Fly Venus and phlebotomy, for they are neither good.
Now little fish on tender stone begin to cast their bellies,
And sluggish snails, that erst were mute, do creep out of
    their shellies.
The rumbling rivers now do warm for little boys to paddle.
The sturdy steed, now goes to grass, and up they hang
    his saddle.
The heavy hart, the bellowing buck, the rascal and the
    pricket,
Are now among the yeoman's peas, and leave the fearful
    thicket.
And be like them, oh you, I say, of this same noble town,
And lift aloft your velvet heads, and, slipping off your gown,
With bells on legs and napkins clean unto your shoulders
    tide,
With scarfs and garters as you please, and 'Hey for our
    town' cried,
March out and show your willing minds, by twenty and
    by twenty,
To Hogsdon or to Newington, where ale and cakes are
    plenty.
And let it here be said for shame that we, the youths
    of London,
Lay thrumming of our caps at home, and left our custom
    undone.
Up then, I say, both young and old, both man and maid
    a-maying

With drums and guns that bounce aloud, and merry tabor
    playing.
Which to prolong, God save our king, and send his
    country peace,
And root out treason from the land; and so, my friends,
    I cease.

ACT V

Enter VENTUREWELL.

VENTUREWELL. I will have no great store of company at
the wedding, a couple of neighbours and their wives, and
we will have a capon in stewed broth, with marrow, and a
good piece of beef, stuck with rosemary.

[*Enter* JASPER, *his face mealed.*]

JASPER. Forbear thy pains, fond man, it is too late.

VENTUREWELL. Heaven bless me! Jasper?

JASPER. Ay, I am his ghost
 Whom thou hast injured for his constant love,
 Fond worldly wretch, who dost not understand
 In death that true hearts cannot parted be.
 First know thy daughter is quite born away
 On wings on angels, through the liquid air,
 To far out of thy reach, and never more
 Shalt thou behold her face. But she and I
 Will in another world enjoy our loves,
 Where neither father's anger, poverty,
 Nor any cross that troubles earthly men
 Shall make us sever our united hearts.
 And never shalt thou sit or be alone
 In any place but I will visit thee
 With ghastly looks, and put into thy mind
 The great offences which thou didst to me.
 When thou art at thy table with thy friends,
 Merry in heart, and filled with swelling wine,

I'll come in midst of all thy pride and mirth,
Invisible to all men but thyself,
And whisper such a sad tale in thine ear
Shall make thee let the cup fall from thy hand,
And stand as mute and pale as Death itself.

VENTUREWELL. Forgive me, Jasper. Oh! what might I do,
Tell me, to satisfy thy troubled ghost?

JASPER. There is no means; too late thou thinkst on this.

VENTUREWELL. But tell me what were best for me to do?

JASPER. Repent thy deed, and satisfy my father,
And beat fond Humphrey out of thy doors.

[*Exit* JASPER.]

[*Enter* HUMPHREY.]

WIFE. Look, George, his very ghost would have folks beaten.

HUMPHREY. Father, my bride is gone, fair Mistress Luce.
My soul's the font of vengeance, mischief's sluice.

VENTUREWELL.
Hence, fool, out of my sight, with thy fond passion!
Thou hast undone me!

[*He beats* HUMPHREY.]

HUMPHREY.   Hold, my father dear,
For Luce thy daughter's sake, that had no peer.

VENTUREWELL.
Thy father, fool? There's some blows more, begone!
Jasper, I hope thy ghost be well appeased
To see thy will performed. Now I will go
To satisfy thy father for thy wrongs.

[*Exit.*]

HUMPHREY. What shall I do? I have been beaten twice.
  And Mistress Luce is gone. Help me, device.
  Since my true love is gone, I nevermore,
  Whilst I do live, upon the sky will pore,
  But in the dark will wear out my shoe-soles
  In passion in Saint Faith's Church under Paul's.

  [*Exit.*]

WIFE. George, call Rafe hither. If you love me, call Rafe
  hither. I have the bravest thing for him to do, George.
  Prithee, call him quickly

CITIZEN. Rafe, why Rafe, boy!

  [*Enter* RAFE.]

RAFE. Here, sir.

CITIZEN. Come hither, Rafe. Come to thy mistress, boy.

WIFE. Rafe, I would have thee call all the youths together in
  battle'ray, with drums, and guns and flags, and march to
  Mile End in pompous fashion, and there exhort your
  soldiers to be merry and wise, and to keep their beards
  from burning, Rafe, and then skirmish and let your flags
  fly, and cry 'Kill, kill, kill'. My husband shall lend you his
  jerkin, Rafe, and there's a scarf. For the rest, the house
  shall furnish you, and we'll pay for't. Do it bravely, Rafe,
  and think before whom you perform and what person you
  represent.

RAFE. I warrant you, Mistress, if I do it not for the honor of
  the City and the credit of my master, let me never hope
  for freedom.

WIFE. 'Tis well spoken, i'faith. Go thy ways, thou art a spark
  indeed.

CITIZEN. Rafe, double your files bravely, Rafe.

RAFE. I warrant you, sir,

[*Exit* RAFE.]

CITIZEN. Let him look narrowly to his service, I shall take him else. I was there myself a pikeman once, in the hottest of the day, wench; had my feather shot sheer away, the fringe of my pike burnt off with powder, my pate broken with a scouring-stick, and yet I thank God I am here.

[*Drum within.*]

WIFE. Hark, George, the drums.

CITIZEN. Ran, tan, tan, tan, ran tan! Oh, wench, an thou hadst but seen little Ned of Aldgate, Drum Ned, how he made it roar again, and laid on like a tyrant, and then struck softly till the ward came up, and then thundered again, and together we go. 'Sa, sa, sa, bounce', quoth the guns, 'Courage, my hearts', quoth the captains, 'Saint George', quoth the pikemen, and withal here they lay, and there they lay: And yet for all this I am here, wench.

WIFE. Be thankful for it George, for indeed 'tis wonderful.

[*Enter* RAFE *and his company, with drums and colours.*]

RAFE. March fair, my hearts. Lieutenant, beat the rear up. Ancient, let your colours fly – but have a great care of the butcher's hooks at Whitechapel, they have been the death of many a fair ancient. Open your files that I may take a view both of your persons and munition. Sergeant, call a muster.

SERGEANT. A stand! William Hamerton, pewterer!

HAMERTON. Here, captain.

RAFE. A corslet and a Spanish pike; 'tis well. Can you shake
it with a terror?

HUMPHREY. I hope so, captain.

RAFE. Charge upon me.
[HAMERTON *charges* RAFE.]
'Tis with the weakest. Put more strength, William
Hamerton, more strength. As you were again. Proceed,
sergeant.

SERGEANT. George Greengoose, poulterer!

GREENGOOSE. Here.

RAFE. Let me see your piece, neighbour Greengoose. When
was she shot in?

GREENGOOSE. An't like you, master captain, I made a
shot even now, partly to scour her and partly for audacity.

RAFE. It should seem so certainly, for her breath is yet
inflamed. Besides, there is a main fault in the touch-hole, it
runs and stinketh, and I tell you, moreover, and believe it,
ten such touch-holes would breed the pox in the army. Get
you a feather, neighbour. Get you a feather, sweet oil and
paper and your piece may do well enough yet. Where's
your powder?

GREENGOOSE. Here.

RAFE. What, in a paper? As I am a soldier and a gentleman,
it craves a martial court. You ought to die for't. Where's
your horn? Answer me to that.

GREENGOOSE. An't like you, sir, I was oblivious.

RAFE. It likes me not it should be so. 'Tis a shame for you
and a scandal to all our neighbours, being a man of worth

and estimation, to leave your horn behind you. I am afraid
'twill breed example. But let me tell you no more on't; stand,
till I view you all. What's become o'th' nose of your flask?

1st SOLDIER. Indeed, la, captain, 'twas blown away with
powder.

RAFE. Put on a new one at the city's charge. Where's the
stone of this piece?

2nd SOLDIER. The drummer took it out to light tobacco.

RAFE. 'Tis a fault, my friend, put it in again. You want a
nose, and you a stone – sergeant, take a note on't, for I
mean to stop it in the pay. Remove and march! Soft and
fair, gentlemen, soft and fair! Double your files! As you
were! Faces about! Now, you with the sodden face, keep in
there! Look to your match, sirrah, it will be in your fellow's
flask anon. So, make a crescent now! Advance your pikes!
Stand and give ear! Gentlemen, countrymen, friends and
my fellow-soldiers, I have brought you this day from the
shops of security and the counters of content to measure
out in these furious fields honour by the ell and prowess by
the pound. Let it not, oh, let it not, I say, be told hereafter
the noble issue of this city fainted, but bear yourselves in
this fair action like men, valiant men, and free men. Fear
not the face of the enemy, nor the noise of the guns, for
believe me, brethren, the rude rumbling of a brewer's car
is more terrible, of which you have a daily experience.
Neither let the stink of powder offend you, since a more
valiant stink is nightly with you. To a resolved mind, his
home is everywhere. I speak not this to take away the
hope of your return, for you shall see, I do not doubt it,
and that very shortly, your loving wives again, and your
sweet children, whose care doth bear you company in
baskets. Remember, then, whose cause you have in hand,
and like a sort of true-born scavengers, scour me this

famous realm of enemies. I have no more to say but this: stand to your tacklings, lads, and show to the world you can as well brandish a sword as shake an apron. Saint George and on, my hearts!

ALL. Saint George! Saint George!

[*Exit.*]

WIFE. 'Twas well done, Rafe, I'll send thee a cold capon a-field, and a bottle of March beer, and, it may be, come myself to see thee.

CITIZEN. Nell, the boy hath deceived me much, I did not think it had been in him. He has performed such a matter, wench, that if I live, next year I'll have him captain of the galley-foist or I'll want my will.

[*Enter* OLD MERRYTHOUGHT.]

OLD MERRYTHOUGHT. Yet, I thank God, I break not a wrinkle more than I had. Not a stoop, boys? Care live with cats, I defie thee! My heart is as sound as an oak, and though I want drink to wet my whistle, I can sing. [*Sings.*]
Come no more there, boys, come no more there,
For we shall never whilst we live, come any more there.

[*Enter a* BOY *with a coffin.*]

BOY. God save you, sir.

OLD MERRYTHOUGHT. It's a brave boy. Can'st thou sing?

BOY. Yes, sir, I can sing, but 'tis not so necessary at this time.

OLD MERRYTHOUGHT [*sings*].
Sing we, and chant it,
Whilst love doth grant it.

BOY. Sir, sir, if you knew what I have brought you, you would have little list to sing.

OLD MERRYTHOUGHT [*sings*].
>   *Oh, the minion round,*
>   *Full long I have thee sought.*
>   *And now I have thee found,*
>   *And what hast thou here brought?*

BOY. A coffin, sir, and your dead son Jasper in it.

OLD MERRYTHOUGHT. Dead? [*Sings.*]
>   *Why, farewell he.*
>   *Thou wast a bonny boy*
>   *And I did love thee.*

[*Enter* JASPER.]

JASPER. Then I pray you, sir, do so still.

OLD MERRYTHOUGHT. Jasper's ghost? [*Sings.*]
>   *Thou art welcome from Stygian lake so soon.*
>   *Declare to me what wondrous things in Pluto's court are done.*

JASPER. By my troth, sir, I ne'er came there. 'Tis too hot for me, sir.

OLD MERRYTHOUGHT. A merry ghost, a very merry ghost. [*Sings.*]
>   *And where is your true love? Oh, where is yours?*

JASPER. Marry, look you, sir.

[*He heaves up the coffin and* LUCE *climbs out.*]

OLD MERRYTHOUGHT. Aha! Art thou good at that i'faith? [*Sings.*]
>   *With hey, trixy, terlery-whiskin,*
>   *The world it runs on wheels,*
>   *When the young man's – – ,*
>   *Up goes the maiden's heels.*

[MISTRESS MERRYTHOUGHT *and* MICHAEL *within.*]

MISTRESS MERRYTHOUGHT. What, Master
Merrythought, will you not let's in? What do you think
shall become of us?

OLD MERRYTHOUGHT. What voice is that that calleth at
our door?

MISTRESS MERRYTHOUGHT [*within*]. You know me well
enough. I am sure I have not been such a stranger to you.

OLD MERRYTHOUGHT [*sings*].
And some they whistled, and some they sung,
Hey down, down,
And some loudly say,
Ever as the Lord Barnet's horn blew,
Away, Musgrave, away.

MISTRESS MERRYTHOUGHT [*within*]. You will not have
us starve here, will you, Master Merrythought?

JASPER. Nay, good sir, be persuaded. She is my mother. If
her offences have been great against you, let your own love
remember she is yours, and so forgive her.

LUCE. Good master Merrythought, let me entreat you. I will
not be denied.

MISTRESS MERRYTHOUGHT [*within*]. Why, Master
Merrythought, will you be a vexed thing still?

OLD MERRYTHOUGHT. Woman, I take you to my love
again, but you shall sing before you enter. Therefore
dispatch your song and so come in.

MISTRESS MERRYTHOUGHT [*within*]. Well, you must
have your will when all's done. Mick, what song canst thou
sing, boy?

MICHAEL. I can sing none, forsooth, but 'A Lady's
Daughter of Paris' properly.

MISTRESS MERRYTHOUGHT & MICHAEL [*within, sing*].
It was a ladies daughter, &c.

OLD MERRYTHOUGHT. Come, you're welcome home
again. [*Sings.*]
If such danger be in playing,
And jest must to earnest turn,
You shall go no more a-maying.

VENTUREWELL [*within*]. Are you within, sir? Master
Merrythought?

JASPER. It is my master's voice. Good sir, go hold him talk
whilst we convey our selves into some inward room.

OLD MERRYTHOUGHT. What are you? Are you merry?
You must be very merry if you enter.

VENTUREWELL. I am, sir.

OLD MERRYTHOUGHT. Sing, then.

VENTUREWELL. Nay, good sir, open to me.

OLD MERRYTHOUGHT. Sing, I say, or by the merry
heart, you come not in.

VENTUREWELL. Well, sir, I'll sing. [*Sings.*]
Fortune my foe, &c.

OLD MERRYTHOUGHT. You are welcome, sir, you are
welcome. You see your entertainment, pray you be merry.

VENTUREWELL.
Oh, Master Merrythought, I am come to ask you
Forgiveness for the wrongs I offered you
And your most virtuous son. They're infinite.

Yet my contrition shall be more than they.
I do confess my hardness broke his heart,
For which just heaven hath given me punishment
More than my age can carry. His wandering spirit,
Not yet at rest, pursues me every where,
Crying, 'I'll haunt thee for thy cruelty'.
My daughter, she is gone, I know not how,
Taken invisible, and whether living
Or in grave, 'tis yet uncertain to me.
Oh, Master Merrythought, these are the weights
Will sink me to my grave. Forgive me, sir.

OLD MERRYTHOUGHT. Why, sir, I do forgive you, and
be merry.
And if the wag in's lifetime played the knave,
Can you forgive him too?

VENTUREWELL.   With all my heart, sir.

OLD MERRYTHOUGHT.
Speak it again, and heartily.

VENTUREWELL.   I do, sir.
Now, by my soul, I do.

OLD MERRYTHOUGHT [*sings*].
With that came out his paramour,
She was as white as the lily flower,
Hey trolly, trolly, lolly.

[*Enter* LUCE *and* JASPER.]

With that came out her own dear knight,
He was as true as ever did fight, &c.
Sir, if you will forgive 'em, clap their hands together.
There's no more to be said i'th' matter.

VENTUREWELL. I do, I do.

CITIZEN. I do not like this. Peace boys, hear me, one of you. Everybody's part is come to an end but Rafe's, and he's left out.

BOY. 'Tis long of your self, sir. We have nothing to do with his part.

CITIZEN. Rafe, come away. Make on him as you have done of the rest, boys, come.

WIFE. Now, good husband, let him come out and die.

CITIZEN. He shall, Nell. Rafe, come away quickly and die, boy.

BOY. 'Twill be very unfit he should die, sir, upon no occasion, and in a comedy, too.

CITIZEN. Take you no care for that, sir boy. Is not his part at an end, think you, when he's dead? Come away, Rafe.

[*Enter* RAFE, *with a forked arrow through his head.*]

RAFE. When I was mortal, this my costive corpse
　　Did lap up figs and raisins in the Strand,
　　Where sitting, I espied a lovely dame
　　Whose master wrought with lingel and with awl,
　　And under ground he vamped many a boot.
　　Straight did her love prick forth me, tender sprig,
　　To follow feats of arms in warlike wise,
　　Through Waltham Desert, where I did perform
　　Many achievements and did lay on ground
　　Huge Barbaroso, that insulting giant,
　　And all his captives soon set at liberty.
　　Then honour pricked me from my native soil
　　Into Moldavia, where I gained the love
　　Of Pompiana, his beloved daughter,
　　But yet proved constant to the black-thumbed maid

Susan and scorned Pompiana's love.
Yet liberal I was and gave her pins,
And money for her father's officers,
I then returned home and thrust myself
In action, and by all means chosen was
The Lord of May, where I did flourish it
With scarfs and rings, and posy in my hand.
After this action I preferred was,
And chosen city captain at Mile End,
With hat and feather, and with leading-staff,
And trained my men, and brought them all off clear,
Save one man that berayed him with the noise.
But all these things I, Rafe, did undertake
Only for my beloved Susan's sake.
Then coming home, and sitting in my shop
With apron blue, Death came unto my stall
To cheapen *aqua vitae*. But ere I
Could take the bottle down and fill a taste,
Death came and caught a pound of pepper in his hand
And sprinkled all my face and body o'er,
And in an instant vanished away.

CITIZEN. 'Tis a pretty fiction, i'faith.

RAFE. Then took I up my bow and shaft in hand
And walked in Moorfields to cool myself.
But there grim cruel Death met me again
And shot this forked arrow through my head,
And now I faint. Therefore be warned by me,
My fellows every one, of forked heads.
Farewell all you good boys in merry London,
Ne'er shall we more upon Shrove Tuesday meet
And pluck down houses of iniquity.
My pain increaseth. I shall never more
Hold open, whilst another pumps both legs,

Nor daub a satin gown with rotten eggs –
Set up a stake, oh, never more I shall.
I die. Fly, fly my soul to Grocers Hall.
Oh, oh, oh, &c.

WIFE. Well said, Rafe, do your obeisance to the gentlemen
and go your ways. Well said, Rafe.

[*Exit* RAFE.]

OLD MERRYTHOUGHT. Methinks all we, thus kindly and
unexpectedly reconciled, should not part without a song.

VENTUREWELL. A good motion.

OLD MERRYTHOUGHT. Strike up, then.

SONG.
Better music ne'er was known
Than a choir of hearts in one.
Let each other that hath been
Troubled with the gall or spleen
Learn of us to keep his brow
Smooth and plain as yours are now.
Sing, though before the hour of dying
He shall rise, and then be crying,
'Hey ho, 'tis nought but mirth,
That keeps the body from the earth'.

[*Exit.*]

Epilogue

CITIZEN. Come, Nell. shall we go? The play's done.

WIFE. Nay, by my faith, George, I have more manners than
so. I'll speak to these gentlemen first. I thank you all,
gentlemen, for your patience and countenance to Rafe, a
poor fatherless child, and if I may see you at my house, it
should go hard but I would have a pottle of wine and a
pipe of tobacco for you. For, truly, I hope you like the
youth but I would be glad to know the truth. I refer it to
your own discretions, whether you will applaud him or no,
for I will wink, and whilst you shall do what you will, I
thank you with all my heart. God give you good night.
Come, George.

Glossary

Aby – pay for

Agricola – probably a mispronunciation of Agriola, a heroine from the romance *Palmerin d'Oliva*

Amadis de Gaul – hero of a romance of the same title

Ancient – aide, advisor

Avernus – lake in Italy reputed to be the gateway to Hades

Barbarian – literally from Barbary

Basted – beat

Bate – rebate

Beray – befoul

Bevis – hero of the romance *Sir Bevis of Hampton*

Bezzle – embezzle

Brionella – character in the romance *Palmerin d'Oliva*

Bullets – small soap pellets

Buss – kiss

Caitiff – rogue, or roguish

Cap – arrest

Carduus benedictus – blessed thistle, a herbal remedy

Cark – worry

Coined – fabricated, often illegally

Condign – apt

Cony – rabbit

Copper basin on a prickant spear – traditional sign denoting a barber-surgeon's shop

Corslet – part of suit of armour covering the body

Costive – constipated

Dagonet – King Arthur's jester

Denier – French coin of low value

Devoir – duty, obligation

Ding – strike with a sword point; colloquially, a jibe

Double gelding – horse for two riders

Double jug – strong form of beer

Dragon's water – remedy against fever

Ell – measure of forty five inches

Enow – enough

Ettins – giants, German mythology

Factor – factotum, agent

Fading – a dance

Featously – with agility

Fegaries – jokes, pranks

Fire-drake – dragon

Flappet – small flap, as in a shop counter

Flirt-gill – flirter

Foul chive – ill betide

Frannarco – giant in the romance *Palmerin d'Oliva*

Froward – contrary

Galley-foist – ceremonial barge

Gargantua – hero of Rabelais's tale of the same name

Gaskins – knee breeches

Gent – of gentle birth

Girds – sneers

Groutnoll – blockhead

Halter-sack – one destined to hang

Hight – called

Hoiting – roistering

Huffing – overblown, bombastic

Ingrant – ignorant

Iwis – certainly

Jeronimo – version of Hieronimo, the hero of Thomas Kyd's
    play *The Spanish Tragedy*

John Dory – hero of a popular song of the time

Knacks – knick-knacks

Lavolta – lively dance

Lay – bet

Lets – obstacles

Lingel – cobblers' thread

List – want, desire

Lungies – corruption of Longinus, the soldier who pierced
    Christ's side with a spear; colloquially, a lout

March beer – strong, long-fermented beer

Master Monkster – probably Richard Mulcaster, former master
    of the Children of the King's Revels, a rival to the
    company that staged Beaumont's play.

Mirror – exemplar

Mithridatum – medicine supposedly effective against poisons

Mittimus – legal Latin, 'We send'; a warrant for arrest

Nice – over-fastidious

Ninevie – corruption of 'Nineveh', where Jonah preached after
    escaping the whale, a tale which was the theme of a
    popular puppet show of the time

Nipitato – strong ale

Nump – fool

Palmer – pilgrim

Palmerin of England – a romance

Peccavi – Latin; 'I have sinned'

Pece – cup

Peppernel – lump, as from a blow

Periwig – wig

Pitch-field – battle

Pluck a rose – urinate

Points – clothing ties

Portigo – Portugal

Pottle – jug containing four British pints

Powdered – corned, salted

Prest – willing, prepared

Prickant – erect

Pricket – young deer

Pricking – spurring

Rebeck – bowed string instrument

Reparel – apparel

Rosicleer – hero of the romance *The Mirror of Knighthood*

Scorched – slashed

Shawm – double-reeded wind instrument

Shroadly – seriously

Snick up – hang (oneself)

Spaniels – Spaniards

Springald – youngster

Squire of Damsels – character in Edmund Spenser's allegorical romance *The Faerie Queene*

Staples – warehouses or markets

Strait – tight

Stringer – fornicator

Stoup – jar or cask, typically for alcohol

Swaddle – beat

Swinge – beat

Tabor – drum

Take – berate

Tartarian – mispronunciation of Sextus Tarquinus, the villain of *The Rape of Lucrece*

Trained – lured

Trim – remove rough edges; colloquially, to beat

Troll – pass

Vale – farewell

Vamped – revamped, repaired

Waits – publicly maintained musical band

Wanion – vengeance

Wastethrift – spendthrift

Wight – person

Won – dwell

Ycleped – named